George + Margaret Feiger

December 1974

D1588169

ANTICIPATIONS, UNCERTAINTY, AND DYNAMIC PLANNING

ANTICIPATIONS, UNCERTAINTY, AND DYNAMIC PLANNING

By

ALBERT GAILORD HART

Professor of Economics
Columbia University

REPRINTS OF ECONOMIC CLASSICS

AUGUSTUS M. KELLEY · PUBLISHER
NEW YORK · 1965

LIBRARY OF CONGRESS CATALOGUE CARD NUMBER

51 - 5465

PREFACE TO 1951 EDITION

FOR generations, economists have had in mind Jevons's dictum that "bygones are forever bygones". The past, then, is dead; the present exists only as a hairline between past and future, important as the locus of decisions; these decisions (and hence the content of economics) refer to the future. But this is not the impression a hasty reader would get from the neo-classical micro-economics—most of which is written in a sort of double-talk, which does not bring to the surface the futurity of the quantities entering economic calculation.

So long as the problem of economic fluctuations was only one corner of the profession's interests, this peculiarity of our central line of theoretical thinking was not very bothersome. But as events of the 1930's made fluctuations our chief focus of interest, a number of Anglo-American economists (as well as the Swedes who had pioneered in this field), found themselves forced to reformulate their micro-economics in terms of anticipations.[1] The monograph here reprinted was part of the rather substantial literature this approach produced between 1935 and 1940.

The problem became acute for me in the winter of 1930-31, in Vienna, when I was forced to think hard about the questions raised in Hayek's 1931 London lectures—which were published as *Prices and Production*.[2] I had been indoctrinated with the anticipations standpoint in my undergraduate days by F. W. Taussig's insistence that the lag between input and corresponding output made it necessary to handle imputation problems in terms of *discounted* marginal productivity. This approach was made still more natural by the concentration of the "trio seminar" of Haberler, Hayek and Morgenstern in Vienna in the autumn of 1930 upon Fisher's *Theory of Interest*. The insis-

---

[1] Gunnar Myrdal's doctoral dissertation (*Prisbildnings-Problemet och Föränderligheten,* Uppsala: Almquist & Wiksell, 1927), still remains untranslated, and probably would still have a good deal to say to us.

In the United States, C. F. Roos published in 1925-1934 a series of writings which he asserts "pioneered and abandoned" the expectational approach. Rereading of the most accessible of his early papers (*Journal of Political Economy,* October 1927 and October 1930) confirms that he described the firm as maximizing discounted profit.

[2] F. A. Hayek, *Prices and Production,* London: George Routledge and Sons, 1931. It was always my feeling that this publication was premature, some of the most interesting points in the lectures being suppressed because they were incompletely worked out.

tence of the students in the seminar on reformulating Fisher in terms of Böhm-Bawerk (!) gave plenty of exercise in input-output lags. When confronted with Hayek's business cycle theory, I found I could not be either for it or against it without new constructions. In particular, I had to figure out what happened if the firms in a given "vertical segment" had inconsistent expectations.[3]

These questions were a focus of discussion among the graduate students at Chicago in 1931-34, and not unnaturally led me to a dissertation topic. Setting out with an ambitious project for a complete "Monetary Theory of Capital", I found myself focussing more and more on the dynamics of expectations in the firm.[4] In the autumn of 1934, when I arrived at the London School of Economics with a rough draft under my arm (written just after landing in England[5]), I found a lively discussion in progress. J. R. Hicks was just preparing the lectures which became his article on "Wages and Interest—the Dynamic Problem."[6] Shortly, there was circulated a mimeograph from Erik Lindahl, anticipating a key section of his later *Money and Capital*.[7] In this atmosphere, I rounded off in December 1934 my first reasonably complete draft of the material which went into this monograph. After various vicissitudes,[8] my disserta-

---

[3] Hayek himself came presently to put a good deal of stress on this issue; see his comment (in an article whose original form dates from 1933) in "Price Expectations, Monetary Disturbances and Maladjustments" (American Economic Association, *Readings in Business Cycle Theory*, Philadelphia: Blakiston, 1944, p. 354).

[4] Turning over my files, I find three stages of work in 1933. A 40-page "Prospectus for PhD Thesis" dated August (and bearing rather drastic critical notes from F. H. Knight) developed into a first-draft text of several chapters on business cycles with outlines for many more (dated October). Then came a more chastened "Prospectus for PhD Thesis on Reduced Scale", dated November, and dealing with the economics of the firm and of the Hayekian "vertical segment". This contained in tabloid form a large proportion of the analysis which eventually appeared in this monograph.

[5] This draft (dated October 1934, and annotated by Hayek) has 85 pages on the firm—plus signs of a revival of over-ambitious ideas in the form of a "prospectus for thesis on a large scale".

[6] *Economic Journal*, 1935, pp. 456-468. This material later blossomed into chapters 15-17 of J. R. Hick's *Value and Capital* (Oxford: Clarendon Press, 1939).

[7] London: George Allen & Unwin, 1939, pp. 74-136.

[8] For the comfort of this generation of graduate students, let me mention that the draft finally accepted as a dissertation was the fifth or sixth for most chapters; the committee (consisting of F. H. Knight, Henry Schultz, Jacob Viner and T. O. Yntema) put me through two full drafts, representing a year's work, after the draft I deluded myself was final!

The diagrams of the final draft (of which one appears on p. 58 of the monograph) were by the redoubtable Dr. Wong—the mathematician with whom Jacob Viner (on a celebrated occasion) could not agree about the envelope curve.

tion was accepted at the University of Chicago in the spring of 1936. Various offshoots of it got into print during 1936-37.[9] This monograph, published in 1940, was a revision of the parts of the dissertation dealing most specifically with the firm.[10]

In view of the size of the vacuum in the theoretical structure which the anticipations analysis was aimed to fill, one might have expected it by 1950 to be a very prominent part of economics. While only a minority of Anglo-American theorists were working on it, that minority included a number of fresh and powerful minds—notably J. R. Hicks, Moses Abramovitz[11], Jacob Marschak[12], Gerhard Tintner[13], and G. L. S. Shackle[14]. We had the advantage of a number of promising leads from Irving Fisher, from J. M. Keynes, and from the Swedish pioneers of the expectational point of view—in part directly, in part through the series of first-rate Swedish travelling fellows. Yet our hopes of developing a formal dynamic theory organized around anticipations do not seem to be panning out. Of the group named above, only Shackle has produced a postwar book along these lines.[15] J. R. Hicks, whose *Value and Capital* was the high-water mark of expectational economics in English before

---

[9] "Anticipations, Business Planning and the Cycle" (*Quarterly Journal of Economics*, February 1937, pp. 272-293) carried the title of the dissertation and constituted its "essential portions". This was a summary.

In addition, "Failure and Fulfillment of Expectations in Business Fluctuations" (*Review of Economic Statistics*, May 1937) gave a fuller account of the part of the analysis dealing with inter-firm relations—influenced particularly by Lindahl. This was developed and applied in "Consumption Markets" (*American Economic Review* Supplement, March 1938, pp. 113-125).

A sideline was my paper on "Imputation and Demand for Productive Resources in Disequilibrium", in the volume in honor of F. W. Taussig (*Explorations in Economics*, New York: McGraw-Hill, 1936, pp. 264-271).

[10] The change of title was to avoid library-catalogue confusion with the "essential portions", and to differentiate the monograph, which largely omitted the topic of inter-firm relations.

Written in late 1940, but published in 1942 was a paper on "Risk, Uncertainty, and the Unprofitability of Compounding Probabilities", in the volume in memory of Henry Schultz (reprinted by American Economic Association in *Readings in the Theory of Income Distribution*, Philadelphia: Blakiston, 1946, pp. 547-557).

[11] *Price Theory for a Changing Economy*, New York: Columbia University Press, 1939.

[12] "Assets, Prices and Monetary Theory", *Economica*, August 1938, pp. 261-288.

[13] "Maximization of Utility over Time", *Econometrica*, April 1938, pp. 154-158; "Non-Static Theory of Choice", *Quarterly Journal of Economics*, February 1942, pp. 274-306: "Theory of Production under Nonstatic Conditions", *Journal of Political Economy*, October 1942, pp. 645-667.

[14] *Expectations, Investment and Income*. London: Oxford University Press, 1938.

[15] *Expectation in Economics*. Cambridge: Cambridge University Press, 1949.

the war, has nothing to add on the subject in his 1946 edition, and scarcely mentions anticipations in his *Contribution to the Theory of the Trade Cycle*.[16] Ingvar Svennilson's *Ekonomisk Planering*[17] (of which I for one would greatly value a translation) has not been followed up. Anticipations play no significant role in the ambitious dynamics of R. F. Harrod[18] and B. S. Keirstead.[19] When the American Economic Association assigned P. A. Samuelson to report on the progress of dynamic economics, the result was an essay on the logic and applications of differential equations, with no discussion of anticipations anywhere visible.[20]

The fact that the expectational approach has not raised the flag of sovereignty over a large area of formal theory (like the monopolistic-competition approach, or the differential-equation-dynamics approach) goes back, I think, to the difficulty of formalizing the way expectations are formed. If we assume that the framing of expectations is an "endogenous" process—that expectations depend strictly on the previous sequence of economic-quantitative events—and that the pattern is stable, then any formal model will show events as a function of expectations, and expectations as a function of earlier events. In this case, events can be reduced to a function of earlier events.[21] The result is a clearcut "sequence analysis" in which anticipations need not appear explicitly—formally a *mechanical dynamics,* with an *expectational dynamics* between the lines.

If we assume (which for many problems makes more sense) that expectations on the basis of a past sequence of economic quantities are powerfully influenced by politics, inventions, etc., then without bringing in "exogenous" variables we cannot get a clearcut process-analysis sequence. We may assume we know

---

[16] Oxford: Clarendon Press, 1950.

[17] Uppsala: Almquist & Wiksell, 1938.

[18] *Towards a Dynamic Economics.* London: MacMillan, 1948. This was the starting point of Hicks's *Trade Cycle.*

[19] *Theory of Economic Change.* Toronto: MacMillan, 1948.

[20] H. S. Ellis (ed.) *Survey of Contemporary Economics.* Philadelphia: Blakiston, 1948, pp. 352-387.

[21] This process is exemplified by L. R. Klein in *Economic Fluctuations in the United States, 1921-1941* (New York: Wiley, 1950). In the theory of the firm, we start out (pp. 15 ff) with anticipated-profit equations where anticipations are explicit. But presently (p. 18) we "introduce conventions with regard to the transformation from anticipated values to observable values", and by substitution eliminate the anticipations terms.

expectations and plans at the outset; but after a few "periods" the influence of revisions accumulates, so that any long sequence can only be illustrative. The most we can hope for along this line is to show that some types of starting-points will set up "cumulative processes"—sometimes also that such processes will presently reverse themselves. Even the rather loose generalizations about periodicity and amplitude of fluctuations Hicks offers in his *Trade Cycle* threaten to dissolve into mist.

This is a nuisance to theoretical system-builders; also to forecasters. But it does not follow that the anticipations approach should be given up as a blind alley. Quite the contrary. It is proving that monopolistic-competition theory turns on what it is reasonable to expect A to expect B to expect of A. If we drop the idea of explicit theorizing about expectations, we must give up most of the alleged post-marshallian advances in this area. In monetary theory, *uncertainty* grows more and more crucial. Expectational dynamics is essential in any business cycle theory which is not content to remain purely mechanical.[22] The fiction that anticipations and plans are not "observable" is being dissipated by collection of "intentions" data; and the theory of anticipations is needed to frame and interpret such investigations. In short, the theoretical trend of which this monograph is part *is* taking over large areas of economics as its proponents predicted before the war—but by infiltration into the content of economics, rather than by formally revolutionizing its framework.

ALBERT GAILORD HART

New York, December 1950

---

[22] See W. J. Fellner's chapter on "Employment Theory and Business Cycles" in H. S. Ellis (ed.) *Survey*, especially pp. 53-59, 80-86.

PREFACE

THIS essay presents a monographic summary of the theory of the business firm in a form adapted for use in the study of business fluctuations and more generally of "dynamic" problems. With this use in view, attention has been concentrated on the time elements of the firm's planning, with special emphasis on anticipations; the recent refinements of enterprise theory springing from the study of monopolistic competition, important as they are, have been allowed to fall into the background.

In a work of this sort it is much more important to be systematic and accurate than either to be "original" or to trace every thought back to its source. To conserve space and to avoid the complications that result from merging an argument on a subject with an annotated bibliography, the writer has limited himself to a very small number of bibliographical footnotes. But while it is hoped that this essay makes an appreciable new contribution through the analysis of capital-rationing and of flexibility as the law of response to uncertainty, the writer is not aiming to conceal either from himself or from the reader the fact that only a small fraction of the basic ideas employed are in any sense original.

Professors F. W. Taussig, Irving Fisher, F. A. von Hayek, F. H. Knight, Henry Schultz, Jacob Viner, and J. R. Hicks provided through their writings and teaching the background from which this essay springs and in addition did much at various stages from 1931 to the present time to guide the writer's thinking on the problem. The writer is also indebted for suggestions in correspondence and discussion, for criticism of manuscripts and opportunity to examine manuscripts, to K. E. Boulding, R. Calkins, Sune Carlson, V. Edelberg, M. Friedman, N. Kaldor, O. Lange, E.

Lindahl, T. W. Schultz, G. Stigler, G. Tintner, and T. O. Yntema. He is under deep obligation to the University of Chicago, furthermore, for a generous grant of leave in the academic year 1934–35 which enabled him greatly to extend his contacts with economists interested in these questions and which provided leisure for a first attempt to analyze them at length.

ALBERT GAILORD HART

IOWA STATE COLLEGE
October 1940

TABLE OF CONTENTS

CHAPTER I

INTRODUCTION

I. THE FIRM IN DYNAMIC ECONOMICS

ECONOMISTS of all schools hold that the "profit motive" is the driving force of the capitalistic economy. All economic events are composed of acts of persons, operating as agents of economic units: either of households or of business firms.[1] In explaining economic events, therefore, an essential link is always the explanation of the household or business decisions which the agents are carrying out.

The tradition of economic theory of course recognizes this fundamental position of the theory of the economic unit—particularly of the firm. But, in consequence of their preoccupation with "equilibrium," most theorists down to the last few years have confined themselves to the analysis of "timeless" situations —situations remaining unchanged through time—so that no explicit recognition of problems of anticipations has been needed.

As economic theorists in late years have more and more become absorbed in the problem of business fluctuations, the inadequacy of a "timeless" theory of the unit has been generally recognized. If economic theory of traditional type can be brought to bear on business-cycle problems, it must allow for anticipations of change and for uncertainty—that is, for states of mind of those who plan the activities of firms and households influencing their plans.

Recent theoretical literature—particularly since 1930—is rich in suggestions for this revision of the theory of the unit. So far, however, these suggestions have remained scattered and un-co-ordinated. The goal of this essay is to weave them together and to

[1] This implies the traditional abstraction from the role of government in the economy.

develop a theory of the firm[2] which will be serviceable for dynamic analysis of markets and of the economy as a whole.

II. CONCEPT OF THE FIRM

Since the whole essay revolves about the business firm, a working definition is clearly called for at the outset. A *firm*[3] is defined as an organization for business purposes of productive resources under one financial control, exercised by a *capitalist-entrepreneur* (entrepreneur for short). The capitalist-entrepreneur is a person or group of persons making the firm's fundamental decisions—as a minimum, choosing the managing personnel—and putting up enough capital to make the firm financially responsible.[4]

While the entrepreneur by definition must provide part of the firm's capital, he need not be the sole source of financing. The firm may also have bondholders, inactive stockholders or partners, or short-term creditors—providers of capital whose entrepreneurial functions do not go beyond "choosing" the firm's active heads in the sense of not refusing to invest in the concern they control. Active management, including much of the firm's basic planning, may be carried on by employees who are not members of the entrepreneurial group but act in its interest.

In some actual concerns the group putting up the capital which makes the firm financially responsible may be entirely separate from the group making the fundamental decisions. This is sometimes the case in corporations where

[2] For lack of space the writer omits systematic discussion of the theory of the household. See Dr. G. Tintner's articles: "Theoretical Derivation of Dynamic Demand Curves" (*Econometrica*, VI [1938], 375 ff.), "Maximization of Utility over Time" (*ibid.*, pp. 154 ff.), and "Elasticities of Expenditure in the Dynamic Theory of Demand" (*ibid.*, VII [1939], 266 ff.).

[3] *Concern* is used here and there in this essay as a looser term substantially synonymous with "firm." *Enterprise* (noun) is used in a narrower sense, meaning the production or handling of a single homogeneous type of salable output. *Enterprise* (adjective) is used loosely to refer either to a firm or to an enterprise. Cf. K. E. Boulding, "Theory of a Single Enterprise," *Quarterly Journal of Economics*, Vol. XLIX, No. 3 (May, 1935).

[4] This follows F. H. Knight's views on entrepreneurship (see his *Risk, Uncertainty and Profit* [Boston and New York, 1921], *passim*, esp. p. 308; see also B. W. Lewis, "The Corporate Entrepreneur," *Quarterly Journal of Economics*, Vol. LI, No. 3 [May, 1937]).

the power of control is vested in a small class of "voting shares" or in a trustee.

Where this is the case, the concern does not come under this essay's definition of a firm. This should not be regarded as a demerit of the definition, however. The central thread of this essay is the theory of a certain standard pattern of "rational" business planning and activity for a firm. But we must of course be on the alert for grounds of divergence from the standard pattern; and conflicts of interest within concerns which fail to conform to the definition of a firm are peculiarly likely to cause such divergence.

The existence of every firm represents a response to some sort of *business opportunity;* and the fact that the firm is organized about its particular entrepreneur shows that this opportunity is in some way under his control. The opportunity may take any one of a number of forms. It may depend on ownership or lease of an advantageous site. It may represent some measure of control of selling-markets (or buying-markets, or both)—some sort of hold of the entrepreneur over customers or suppliers. It may consist in control of a patented or secret process. Failing any such special opportunity, there must always be, as a minimum, the opportunity to make the most of the entrepreneur's personal services.[5]

The business opportunity of every firm is in some way or other different from that of every other firm; this is what gives firms their identity. Every business opportunity, moreover, has some sort of quantitative limit. The existence of this limit is the fundamental justification for assuming that all firms operate under "diminishing returns to scale." In consequence of it, there is always some maximum-profit scale of operations, short of infinity, for every firm.

Many of the puzzles of the theory of the firm arise from insistence on seeing the limitations of the firm's business opportunity in something which the firm does or can buy. This leads to the well-known paradox that, if all the firm's buying-markets and selling-markets were perfectly competitive, the size of the firm would be indeterminate.[6] Reflection will show, however,

[5] We may take it that the services of a person qualified for entrepreneurship are of higher quality when he is working for himself than when he is an employee—or at least that he values his own services higher than do potential employers (cf. Knight, *op. cit.*, pp. 281 ff.).

[6] See Nicholas Kaldor, "Equilibrium of the Firm," *Economic Journal*, XLIV (March, 1934), 60 ff.

that firms which are not limited by imperfect markets for things they buy are limited by what will be called in chapter iii "rationed free goods."[7] In consequence, it is not necessarily internally inconsistent to assume perfect competition for everything the firm actually buys and sells—as the writer does in the early stages of certain arguments in this essay—so long as we remember that firms use some things they do not buy or sell.[8]

III. "ECONOMIC RATIONALITY"

This essay will follow the tradition of orthodox economic theory in relying upon "rational decisions" by businessmen as motive power for the theoretical engine. But the introduction of anticipations and uncertainty into our problematics makes it necessary to state very carefully just what "economic rationality" implies.[9]

In general terms, the assumption of "rationality" means that every decision is taken for the sake of "the difference it will make" —to quote Professor Viner's phrase—as against alternative decisions whose consequences are likewise estimated. In more technical economic language this amounts to saying that rationality consists in operating on the marginal principle.

But this formula is so very general that it lacks content. We need a more specific criterion of economic rationality, fitting our problem of the firm in a fluctuating world. This involves distinguishing rationality at several levels.

Starting with the level of action and working back into the problem of motivation, we can readily see

a) That rational acts are acts consistent with plans.

b) That rational plans are plans which offer the fullest satisfaction of desired ends attainable with the means at hand, in the light of estimates of the consequences of available alternative lines of action.

c) That rational estimates are estimates built up by correct analysis from the assembled information.

d) That rational assembly of information is assembly on a basis which may reasonably be expected to give a satisfactory approximation to the true state of affairs.

[7] See below, p. 38.

[8] Cf. J. R. Hicks's concept of the "private factors" in "Theory of Monopoly," *Econometrica*, III (1935), 4 ff.

[9] Aside from tradition, "rationality" is not a very good word to characterize what economists have in mind. "Calculatingness" would probably be a more apt expression, if the other were not already the established term.

The logical relations of these different levels are peculiar. Quite plainly, acts cannot be rational in terms of plans unless plans exist; plans cannot be rational unless estimates exist; estimates cannot be rational unless data for estimation are assembled. This would seem to imply that rationality can exist at the action level only if it exists at all the other levels—that postulating rational behavior means postulating rationality at all four levels.

If this inference were correct, it would make the assumption of economic rationality almost absurd; for it is hard to imagine businessmen in general being fully rational either in assembling data of estimation or in forecasting from them. The problem of selecting data is essentially that of statistical sampling—a field in which no procedure is absolutely safe. Costs of inquiry limit observation; but at the same time the different things affecting business prospects are so heterogeneous that restricting observation at all means leaving some classes of relevant facts entirely out of account. The problem of forming estimates from the observations selected is also a knotty one. Arriving at ideal estimates plainly requires knowing all about economics, statistics, and the logic of probability, with a strong dash of psychological, technological, and legal lore thrown in for good measure. The economist, conscious of his own deficient knowledge in all these fields, cannot afford to brand imperfection in the use of these techniques of analysis as "irrational" unless he cares to have his own work so branded.

Fortunately for the economist's peace of mind, however, the successive levels do not make a logical chain. For actions may be rational in the light of irrational plans; plans may be rational in the light of irrational estimates; and estimates may be rational in the light of irrationally selected evidence. We are thus free to assume rationality at some levels without assuming it at others.

Since this essay is concerned chiefly with business plans and only secondarily with actions, it is indifferent whether or not we assume rational action. At the planning level, this essay will follow the theoretical tradition in assuming—aside from certain digressions—that business plans are explicit and are rational in the light of explicit estimates. Neither plans nor estimates need be assumed to be embodied in documents, though either or both may be.[10]

We are under no obligation to make the unplausible assumption that the estimates themselves are fully rational or that businessmen make an ideal selection of data on which to base their estimates. On the other hand, we are not forced to assume that estimates are wholly irrational and arbitrary. For the present all that is necessary at these levels is to guard ourselves against falling into the habit of regarding estimates as bona fide constants in the economic system rather than as parameters which will shift through time in some relation to events.

It should be noted that even at the planning level there is no logical compulsion to assume full rationality (i.e., planning on the marginal principle) in preference to any of a number of patterns of *quasi-rationality*. To give a few samples of the elements from which such patterns might be built up, we might assume:

a) That businessmen arbitrarily exclude from their calculations certain known technical possibilities (e.g., changes in production plans involving variations in the amount of materials used per unit of output).

b) That cost-accounting misleads businessmen into "allocating" all joint costs to particular units of output and that resulting average cost figures (including quotas of inallocable joint costs) are treated as though they were marginal.

c) That businessmen reason marginally in only one direction—that (e.g.) they will raise prices when rising activity raises marginal costs but will not lower prices when their calculated average cost figures at the current output level exceed price, however low the marginal expense at which they could expand output.

d) That businessmen are bad mathematicians and are led to incorrect plans by arithmetical or algebraic errors (including such biased errors as failure to reckon compound interest).

These hypotheses—like many others which might be listed—have a plausible ring; and the variant theories to which they would lead would have a certain claim to superior realism, if used for specific applications. But the writer feels that no combination of such assumptions would have any very broad applicability and that analysis based on a wide variety of quasi-rationality patterns is bound to be confusing. Hence the main stream of

[10] As we shall see later, neither the estimates nor the plans need be assumed *single valued*. In view of uncertainty, both may run in terms of alternative contingencies for the near future and may dissolve into mist in the distant future. See below, pp. 51–55.

argument in this essay assumes full rationality; but at critical places, and with due notice, a few ramifications under assumptions of quasi-rationality are explored.

IV. CONVENIENCES AND LIMITATIONS OF ENTER-PRISE ANALYSIS

In taking the firm as starting-point for dynamic analysis we gain great advantages. The theory of the firm—aside from the problems of anticipations and uncertainty whose treatment is the special object of this essay—is perhaps the most thoroughly explored and best-mapped field of economics. Its central ideas can be traced back at least a hundred years, to Cournot and von Thünen. It has been much in the minds of most English-speaking economists, at least since the appearance of Marshall's *Principles* in 1890; and the post-war discussions of monopolistic competition and (even more) of profit have done much to develop it. Basing our analysis on this tradition thus offers us the foundation of a set of well-tested techniques of analysis, together with an unusually well-standardized outfit of technical terms.

On the other hand, as G. L. S. Shackle has very neatly put it, analysis running from one economic situation to another involves "two stages":

"1. Taking the sets of expectations held by different individuals at one moment as given, ... to show what decisions will be taken at this moment and what will be their immediate consequences, before they are themselves modified in the light of their first effects.

"2. To show how these decisions will in fact be modified after a short interval in the light of their own collective consequences, and thus to build up a chain of situations growing one out of another and representing a process in time."[11]

The theory of the firm, properly developed, can tell us most of what we need to know of the theory of decision-making. The second part of the "first stage"—the tracing of immediate consequences—calls for analysis of interenterprise relations and cannot be handled within the framework of this essay.[12]

[11] *Expectations, Investment and Income* (London, 1938), pp. 1–2.

[12] For examples of such interenterprise analysis (on the whole without adequate allowance for uncertainty) see Hicks, *Value and Capital* (Oxford, 1939), Parts III–IV; E. Lindahl, *Money and Capital* (London, 1939); G. Myrdal, *Monetary Equilib-*

The second stage—the determination of estimates and plans from events—has been obscured in economists' thinking by the habit of speaking of "economic data" as objective facts such as technology, material resources, distribution of property owner-ship, and telescoping the reasoning by which "data" were sup-posed to be shown to determine events. To refuse to attempt the second stage of analysis is to give up trying to motivate accounts of business fluctuations, which is clearly out of the question. Since estimation and planning must obviously happen within the firm, this is also a problem of enterprise theory; and some sugges-tions on it are offered in chapter v below. But for this problem the traditional tool of marginal analysis is useless. The professional competence of the economist—for what it is worth—is in the field where marginal reasoning applies. While economists can hope to make some progress in the formulation of issues in the second stage of analysis, they cannot hope for real solutions until they either develop new techniques or find competent help outside the profession. For the present, therefore, all findings in this field must be considered merely tentative.

---

rium (London, 1939); Shackle, *op. cit.;* and the writer's articles, "Failure and Ful-filment of Expectations in Business Fluctuations" (*Review of Economic Statistics,* Vol. XIX, No. 2 [February, 1937]) and "Consumption Markets" (*American Eco-nomic Review, Supplement,* March, 1938).

CHAPTER II

BUSINESS PLANNING UNDER CERTAINTY

I. PLAN OF THE ESSAY

THE procedure of this essay will be to analyze first the problem of business planning as it would be if the businessman had perfect confidence in his estimates, bringing in uncertainty at a later stage.

The present chapter is based on the assumptions of subjective certainty and of smooth (though not necessarily perfectly competitive) market relations. Chapter iii deals with market discontinuities—rationing, price-fixing, and capital-rationing—still on the assumption of subjective certainty. Chapter iv generalizes the argument to allow for uncertainty, paying particular attention to interrelations between uncertainty and capital-rationing which are important for the theory of money. Chapter v, finally, steps outside the common framework of the first four chapters (in all of which the entrepreneur's estimates are taken as data) and considers the determination of estimates.

II. VARIABLES AND DATA

In the "timeless" enterprise theory of the textbooks the "data" with which the entrepreneur is confronted are market situations (under perfect competition, fixed buying-prices and selling-prices; under monopolistic competition, supply curves and demand curves) and technical input-output relations. These may be thought of as market and technical relations which will rule indefinitely if the firm keeps all its rates of input and output constant.

The "variables" of the situation fall into several groups. Within the limits fixed by technology there is choice as to the level of the various horizontal schedules of input and output. Given the market situation, fixing the rate of flow of any input or output

9

fixes the level of a flow of disbursements or receipts. Given a set of input levels and corresponding output levels, since all disbursements and receipts are determined, there is a corresponding level of net receipts (or gross profits). The object of business planning, under these suppositions, is to find that set of rates of input and output for which net receipts are highest; when operating at these rates, the firm is "in equilibrium."

By the familiar rules of "substitution at the margin," equilibrium operation implies a number of relations among inputs and outputs. Certain output levels might be altered by altering certain input levels in the same direction, or by altering other output levels in the opposite direction—i.e., by substituting input or other output for the output in question; and substitution of inputs for each other is also possible. In equilibrium, however, the net financial effects of all possible substitutions must be neutral or adverse to net receipts. Under standard assumptions large substitutions will be adverse, small substitutions neutral. In "marginal" terms the marginal cost of an extra unit per day of any output must equal its marginal revenue: the change in disbursements implied by the necessary changes in rates of input must just equal the change in receipts implied by the change in rate of output. Similar relations will hold between intersubstitutable outputs and between intersubstitutable inputs.[1]

For purposes of dynamic analysis we need a scheme of things in which possibilities of change through time are recognized. This makes the problem of the firm much more complex than on the "timeless" level. To keep these complexities from becoming unmanageable, it is proposed for the next two chapters to assume that the entrepreneur plans in a world of subjective certainty: that he *thinks he knows* exactly what will happen under every business policy he may contemplate. In the present chapter a further simplification will be made by supposing his buying, selling, and financing to be limited only through prices and effects of prices on prospective profits.

---

[1] For an authoritative and compact statement of the received doctrine see J. R. Hicks, *Value and Capital* (Oxford, 1939), chap. vi.

At the outset we plainly need a working definition of the *business plan*, embodying the entrepreneur's decisions about the variables of the situation under his control.

It is convenient to begin with the production plan, or body of decisions as to physical input and output. Such a plan consists of a set of mutually compatible *production schedules* (definite plans for the amount of salable output of every type produced which shall reach technical completion at each future date) and *input schedules* (plans for the use of various types of productive services at each date). If the firm fabricates intermediate products for its own use, their production schedules must also be included.

The second phase of enterprise planning is the *marketing plan*. This is made up of *buying schedules* for productive services or for durable goods yielding such services and of *sales schedules* for salable output. These schedules are plainly limited—but not rigidly fixed—by the input and production schedules.

The third phase of planning is the *finance plan*. This is made up of *outlay schedules* for disbursements paying for purchases, *receipts schedules* for sales proceeds, a *financing schedule* for receipts and disbursements on capital account from and to persons not in the entrepreneurial group and from and to other firms (including interest payments), and a *withdrawal schedule* for profits paid out to entrepreneurial members (minus receipts from entrepreneurial members investing in the firm).

Each "schedule" may be thought of as a listing of amounts of goods, services, or money which will pass certain checking-stations in each time interval (hour, day, or week, say) beginning with the moment of planning. Alternatively, it may be visualized as a curve in two dimensions, measuring rate of flow through time. If we adopt the latter convention, we may represent a business plan diagrammatically by a set of curves (see Fig. 1), having a common time scale, but each with its separate vertical (rate-of-flow) scale measured in an appropriate unit. The area under each such curve between any pair of dates (such as t_0—the moment of planning—and t_1; see Fig. 1) represents the amount of goods to be

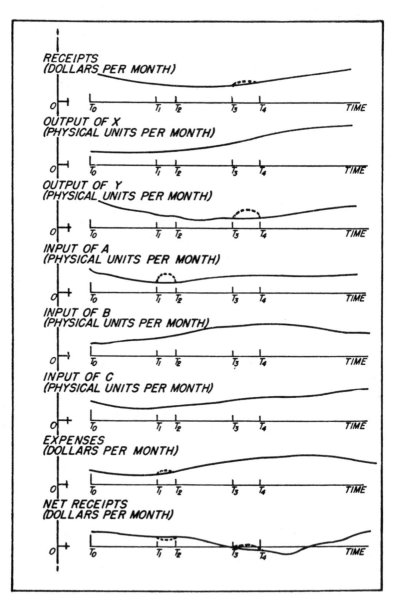

Fig. 1

produced, amount of money to be spent, etc., between those dates under the plan being considered.[2]

The different components of the plan, of course, are interrelated through the firm's *estimates*, which are data in the sense of *data of planning*.[3] These estimates involve both engineering and marketing problems.

Market estimates may be represented graphically by a series of *price schedules*, showing the selling-prices and buying-prices the firm expects to receive and to pay; an *interest schedule* is also needed for refined analysis. If the firm operates under perfect competition as well as perfect certainty, its set of price schedules may be drawn up without reference to its plans of production and marketing. If the firm's markets are not perfectly competitive (so that the firm's choice of marketing plans—perhaps also its program of sales promotion—may affect prices), there must be a special set of price schedules for each contemplated marketing plan. In either case, receipts schedules are to be arrived at by multiplying together for each date the expected selling-price and scheduled sales volume; and similarly for outlay schedules. For every contemplated marketing plan (waiving complications from sales promotion) there must be some one corresponding schedule of total receipts from all lines of sales and of total outlays for all lines of purchases.

There must also be consistency, in the light this time merely of engineering estimates, between input schedules and production schedules. But here there is no question of one-to-one correspondence. A given set of production schedules, in general, could be produced by any of a number of sets of input schedules. Among

[2] The date t_0—the moment when the plan is laid—has a peculiar significance in the theory of enterprise planning. For everything to the left is mere history and no longer under the entrepreneur's control in any respect; while everything to the right is merely planned or contemplated. For convenience, the diagrams of this essay begin at t_0, not showing historical schedules for earlier dates. But this should not be taken to imply that the discussion relates only to new firms; rather, it reflects the economist's traditional view that "bygones are forever bygones" (cf. W. S. Jevons, *Theory of Political Economy* [4th ed.; London, 1911], p. 164).

[3] The *data of estimation*, on which estimates are supposedly based, will be discussed in chap. v below.

production plans which might be adopted, therefore, there are families of plans alike as to output but unlike as to input. The *production function* (i.e., the mass of engineering data which relate the elements of the production plan) cannot be easily expressed by any such system of diagrams as is available for expressing market estimates. Fortunately, however, the diagrammatic difficulties are greater than the logical difficulties involved.

III. CHOICE OF THE OPTIMUM BUSINESS PLAN

In "timeless" enterprise theory it is customary to think of the entrepreneur as seeking to maximize his net receipts—the excess of his gross receipts over his withdrawals. It is proposed in this essay to extend the criterion of maximum net receipts to dynamic planning.[4] But, of course, dollars of different dates are not identical in economic meaning, so that a mere summation of net receipts contemplated for the life of the firm is not significant. Accordingly, the assumption of this chapter is that the entrepreneur lays plans so as to maximize the *present discounted value of scheduled net receipts* for the life of the firm.[5]

The most convenient focus for our analysis is production: we may think of the entrepreneur as drawing up what seems to him a promising set of production schedules (one for each of his types of salable output), and then investigating the corresponding outlays and receipts.

Both on the cost side and on the revenue side, however, his investigation must run in terms of a series of superimposed multiple alternatives. On the cost side they ramify widely:

a) The tentatively adopted set of production schedules may be produced with any of a number of alternative sets of input schedules of productive services.

---

[4] Needless to say, we might adopt other criteria—in particular business income of the firm, or withdrawals of profits from the firm by the entrepreneur. But it happens that all the more attractive competing criteria substantially coincide with the one selected (see Appen., pp. 89–92, below).

[5] The use of the "present" (date of planning) as the base for discounted values is arbitrary and serves chiefly to avoid cumbrous language. In comparing any set of plans, however, shifting the date of valuation will alter all discounted values proportionately, so that nothing is warped by adopting this convention.

b) Each input schedule in each of the alternative sets of (*a*) may ordinarily be provided by any of a number of alternative purchase schedules.

c) Each purchase schedule may ordinarily be financed by any of several alternative outlay schedules.

On the revenue side, in like manner:

d) The tentatively adopted set of production schedules may admit of any of a number of alternative sets of sales schedules.

e) Each sales schedule may commonly be made to yield any of a number of alternative receipts schedules.

The reasons for this ramification of alternatives will bear a brief discussion before we proceed to their resolution. To begin with the cost side, the input alternatives rest simply on the universally recognized possibilities of substituting one type (or date) of input for another. The purchase alternatives for a given input rest on the fact that a flow of productive services is commonly secured through purchase of *sources* of services (service-yielding material goods or immaterial "bundles" of services such as water rights or the labor of employees hired by the month), and that the sources are commonly durable in use or in storage, or both. Only if the services must be bought as such (i.e., if all purchasable sources lack durability either in use or in storage) does the input schedule rigidly determine the purchase schedule. The outlay alternatives, finally, rest on the possibility of varying terms of payment for sources purchased.

The relation between output and receipts is roughly symmetrical with that between input and outlays. For any given production schedule, unless the product lacks durability under storage, there is a range of possible alternative sales schedules. A given sales schedule, in turn, may be made to yield any one of several alternative receipts schedules by varying the terms of sale.

A further source of receipts alternatives springs from the possibility of altering the prices buyers will pay for a given flow of goods, through *sales promotion*. In principle we might complete the symmetry of the scheme by admitting "purchase promotion" to influence buying-prices. But the writer is inclined to follow the theoretical tradition which takes account of the effect of the firm's propaganda on its customers but not on its suppliers. Purchase promotion is possible—witness campaigns to persuade farmers to raise crops neighboring canneries want and efforts to make labor available by selling houses to workers—but, as a matter of degree, it seems plain that it is much less important than sales promotion.

The resolution of this tangle of alternatives is to be found in the principles of least cost and greatest revenue. By their use we can begin at the ends of the chain furthest from production and work back to the tentatively planned production schedules.

In the first place, each of the alternative sets of outlay schedules compatible with a particular contemplated set of purchase schedules can be combined by summation into a *total-outlay schedule* and reduced by discounting to a present value. For the contemplated set of purchase schedules, the best plan of outlays is plainly that with the lowest discounted value; and this lowest-cost plan of outlays can be used to represent the cost of the purchase plan in further calculations, all inferior (higher-cost) outlay plans being dropped from consideration.

On the same principle the different purchase plans compatible with a given plan of input can be compared. For the set of input schedules under contemplation, the lowest-cost purchase plan is to be preferred. The cost of this purchase plan can be used to represent the cost of the input plan, all inferior (higher-cost) purchase plans being dropped from consideration.

The same rule, finally, leads to selection of the best input plan for our contemplated set of production schedules. Again the plan with lowest cost is the best, all inferior (higher-cost) input plans being dropped from consideration. By this process of elimination, the most economical set of input schedules, purchase schedules, and outlay schedules for the set of production schedules under study can be determined.

Turning to the side of receipts, the best system of sales terms and sales promotion for a given contemplated set of sales schedules will be that for which the sum of the receipts schedules (making up the *gross-receipts schedule*)—with deduction of outlays for sales promotion[6]—has the largest present discounted value. This

---

[6] The rule of deducting sales-promotion costs and storage costs from revenue (rather than including them on the cost side) is proposed to preserve the traditional dichotomy of costs and revenues. If we do not adopt it, the whole complex here dealt with must be thrown into one pot: in particular, there is no way of identifying the cost of a given set of production schedules without specifying how it is to be sold. For the comfort of the reader it should be pointed out that any error in allocating costs between production and sales promotion (or storage) will cancel out quantitatively in the final comparison of costs and revenues.

The omission of interest from storage costs is to avoid double counting; it is already provided for by the discounting process.

highest value may be used to represent the revenue from the sales plan in question, all inferior (lower-return) plans of sales promotion being eliminated.

As among the alternative sales plans compatible with the given contemplated production plan, the rule of choice is the same. The sales plan with the highest value of revenue—with further deduction of storage costs, other than interest—is to be preferred. Its corrected value may be taken as the value of the contemplated set of production schedules.

For any contemplated set of production schedules, by following these rules, some unique combination of the alternative sets of input schedules, purchases schedules, outlay schedules, sales schedules, and receipts schedule can be shown to be best. By subtracting outlays at each date from receipts at the same date, a corresponding net-receipts schedule can be worked out; and this can be reduced by discounting to a present value.

Representing each possible set of production schedules by its net-receipts schedule, we may now complete our schematic account of business planning under our present set of assumptions. That production plan will be selected under which the present discounted value of the net-receipts schedule is greatest. This plan, with associated plans for the other magnitudes just listed, will be the *optimum business plan.*

It will be observed that this determination of the optimum plan does not unequivocally determine either the withdrawal schedule or the financing schedule; though it does determine their relation. Neglecting changes in cash balances, withdrawals must be the sum of net receipts and financing obtained. Since all three magnitudes—net receipts, withdrawals, and financing obtained—are capable of negative values, a number of combinations are possible for a given interval. If net receipts are negative, there may be either positive financing (borrowing or sale of stock) or negative withdrawals (investment of funds by entrepreneurs), or both. If net receipts are positive, there must be either negative financing (loan repayment or repurchase of stock) or positive withdrawals.

The *present value* of the financing schedule is a datum of planning which is unchanged from plan to plan: it must always be zero if the firm is out of debt, or minus the firm's present debt where debt exists. The present value of the withdrawal schedule (i.e., the firm's net worth) is given by the present value of net receipts under the optimum plan minus the firm's debt. But the time shape of the withdrawal schedule may be adapted to the preferences of the entrepreneur by borrowing and lending,[7] under our assumption of a free capital market.

IV. THE OPTIMUM PLAN IN MARGINAL TERMS

Like equilibrium of the firm in "static" analysis, the optimum plan under dynamic conditions involves balance among various components of the business plan "at the margin." This implies that alternative business plans shade into one another—that many alternative plans could be constructed, each of which would be identical with the optimum plan except in two or three minor respects. Each difference between such an alternative plan and the optimum plan (or any other plan taken as base) will be spoken of as an *alteration*.[8]

Graphically, such an alteration may be shown by representing two alternative versions of a schedule. The convention used in this chapter is to represent the base schedule under consideration (also the alternative schedule, so far as the two coincide) by a solid curve, the alternative schedule (where the two differ) by a broken curve. A set of related alterations to a contemplated plan may be represented (see Fig. 1) by extending this technique to a diagram showing all the components of the plan in both alternatives.

We may begin by considering the marginal relations existing in a simplified planning problem where storage, sales promotion, etc., are impossible, and where sources of input are not durable in use, so that fixing input determines purchases and outlays, while fixing output determines sales and receipts. For convenience, we may take an output alteration as starting-point, thinking of this alteration as a slight increase in the rate of production of one type of output planned for a short interval of future time (from a date t_3 to a slightly later date t_4).

---

[7] Cf. Irving Fisher, *Theory of Interest* (New York, 1930), chap. v.

[8] "Alteration" is here used in the sense generally given "variation." This shift of terms is necessary, in a dynamic framework, to avoid the temporal connotation of "variation"; for the optimum plan itself presumably contains plans for variation of activities through time.

Under our hypothesis the receipts alteration and output alteration will be simultaneous. The limiting ratio of the former to the
latter—the alteration in receipts per unit alteration in output—is
the *marginal revenue of output*.[9]

We have next to extend the marginal analysis backward into
the fields of input, purchases, and money outlays. To begin with,
it is evident that our supposed upward alteration of the production schedule between t_3 and t_4 (with unchanged technology) must
call for some upward alteration of input schedules. In general,
there will be a number of alternative ways of altering input compatible with the contemplated output alteration. Some of these
input-alteration possibilities *must* be qualitatively and temporally
complex (involving alteration of several input schedules). Some
of them *may* be qualitatively simple, involving alteration of only
one input schedule, between dates t_1 and t_2. Wherever a simple
alteration is possible, a *marginal productivity* can be computed—
i.e., a limiting ratio of the number of physical units of output
added (or subtracted) to the number of physical units of input
added (or subtracted).

In general, each of the possible input alterations will begin and
end before (or at least not later than) the output alteration;
though the two may overlap. Along with any productivity ratio,
therefore, we must think of a time lag. This may conveniently be
expressed by a *reaction interval*, defined as the period extending
from the moment when half the additional input involved in the
input alteration has been used until the moment when half the
additional output involved in the output alteration has appeared.

This reaction interval is the sort of stuff from which—by averaging—
period-of-production concepts are built up. But the present writer sees
neither any satisfactory system of weighting the intervals to be averaged
nor any useful application for the result. The reaction interval is essentially
a marginal concept, whose extension intramarginally (by ascribing reaction
intervals to all input simultaneously instead of alternatively) is illicit.
Furthermore, it is a technological rather than a strictly economic concept;

[9] The limit is taken as the intensity and duration of the output alteration approach zero. This is the "marginal revenue" of the monopolistic competition theorists. The suffix is necessary because we shall presently have need of a concept of
marginal revenue of input.

and, as Dr. Hicks points out,[10] the attempt to use a technological concept of an "average period" leads to error.

It should be noted that the reaction interval is not merely a possible component of an average but itself a relation between averages of a sort—median points of time. So far as the output alteration is concerned, we can get rid of this averaging in the limit by letting its duration approach zero; but it cannot be guaranteed that the duration of the input alteration will also approach zero. If we take the input alteration as base, the situation is still worse. The effect of an input alteration whose duration approaches zero may be a small *permanent* alteration in output. In this event reaction interval and marginal productivity are both infinite; though the present value of the corresponding receipts alteration will still be finite.

A mathematical analysis presented by Dr. Hicks[11] includes expressions which appear to represent the marginal productivity of input of the remote future, expressed in output of the near future, implying the possibility of negative reaction intervals. But he explains these terms as representing deterioration of the firm's plant at early dates, to be repaired later. In short, his scheme of analysis links alterations of output at early dates with alterations of *purchases* at later dates and is not productivity analysis in a strict sense. His position does not imply that output can be altered without altering simultaneous or earlier *use of productive services*. Since "input" in this essay relates to services, no real disagreement is involved.

For each of the alternative input alterations (simple or complex) with which the output alteration can be secured, there must be, under our simplifying assumptions, a simultaneous alteration of purchases and outlays. The limiting ratio of outlay alteration to input alteration is the *marginal cost of input;* and the limiting ratio of outlay alteration to output alteration is the *marginal cost of output*. A separate marginal cost of output can be computed for each alternative way of altering input.

Where simple input alterations are possible, marginal cost of output will equal marginal cost of input divided by marginal productivity. Reciprocally, *marginal revenue of input* will equal marginal revenue of output multiplied by marginal productivity. For complex input alterations the lack of a homogeneous physical unit of input precludes looking at marginal productivity as a simple quantity; but the logic of calculation of marginal cost of output is the same.

[10] *Op. cit.*, pp. 222–23.
[11] "Wages and Interest, the Dynamic Problem," *Economic Journal*, June, 1935.

If the plan under contemplation is really the optimum, no variant plan may offer a higher discounted value of net receipts. This implies that for upward alterations of output all possible input alterations offer marginal costs of output which equal or exceed the marginal revenue of output when both are reduced to discounted dollars of the date of planning. Likewise, for downward output alterations the discounted marginal costs must equal or fall short of the marginal revenue.

The finding that for upward alterations the marginal costs must "equal or exceed" (rather than merely "equal") the marginal revenue reflects two considerations: (1) production may conceivably involve "limitational factors"—i.e., the production function may be such that a given output alteration can always be made more economically by complex than by simple alterations—and (2) "lumpiness" of certain inputs may make very small alterations out of the question; but for large alterations (not strictly "marginal," of course) the optimum plan must obviously be defined by inequalities.

Marginal costs must "equal or fall short of" marginal revenues for downward alterations (rather than "equal or exceed" marginal revenues as with upward alterations) for even more obvious reasons. Present discounted value of net receipts will lose by alteration of the contemplated plan if receipts contract more than costs contract, or if costs expand more than receipts expand; so that the conditions relating to upward and downward alterations from the optimum plan diverge.

Often, it must be recognized, purchased input affects salable output only indirectly, via "intermediate products" produced and used within the firm. In this event the marginal productivity of purchased input—if computable at all—must be computed by a chain process: it is given by the marginal productivity of purchased input in intermediate product times the marginal productivity of intermediate product in terms of salable product.[12]

If we compute marginal productivities by this chain process, the rules above formulated still permit testing whether a given plan is the optimum. Alternatively, we may add the rule that the marginal cost of intermediate products at each date must equal their marginal revenue of input.

[12] Cf. the writer's article on "Imputation and Demand for Productive Resources in Equilibrium," in *Explorations in Economics* (New York: McGraw-Hill, 1936), pp. 264–71.

Reserving our assumption of the absence of durable goods for discussion below, we may readily generalize the argument to allow for the presence of storage and of sales promotion, which have so far been assumed away in this section of the chapter. The process of generalization calls only for the application of rules similar to those of Section II above.

On the output-revenue side we are now obliged to recognize alternative marginal revenues of output for a given output alteration, corresponding to different possible policies as to storage of output, sales promotion, and payment schedules required of customers. But of these alternatives one will plainly have the most favorable present discounted value. For further calculations other alternatives may be discarded and the marginal revenue arising under the preferred sales policy treated as if it were unique.

Similarly on the buying side: Of the alternative alterations of purchases and outlays compatible with a given input alteration, that with the most favorable present value will be preferred and others may be discarded. Application of the rule of most favorable present value thus reduces the problem to the proportions of the simplified problem considered above.

V. VALUATION, PURCHASE, AND PRODUCTION OF DURABLE GOODS

The simplification achieved by assuming the absence of durable goods is more important. The use in production of services of durable goods introduces an element of joint cost as between outputs of different dates. In consequence, calculation of marginal costs corresponding to alterations in the use of these services is blocked.[13] Units of durable goods in use within a firm, moreover, are often few, so that assumptions of continuous variability of input are out of place.

From the standpoint of apportioning the flow of services available from sources on hand, this difficulty is not serious. If use of the services is not postponable, all that is required is equality of

[13] This consideration applies a fortiori to computation of average costs for salable output and is thus a serious barrier to the extension of Marshallian analysis to dynamic problems.

discounted marginal revenue of input in the different uses of the services at each date. If their use is postponable, equality of discounted marginal revenue is required also between dates.

But while these rules are enough to guide the use of services, they do not suffice for all business purposes. They leave the question open when and how far other productive services or cash resources should be used to acquire further sources of services.

The first step toward a remedy is to put a value upon the source by estimating its contribution to the firm. This valuation—which is in the first instance independent of the prices the market offers for the source in question—will be called an *internal value*. Its calculation, however, involves difficulties.

A first approximation may be obtained by calculating the marginal revenue of input of the services at each date over which the source is to be held, thus valuing the flow of services at each date, and taking the total discounted value of the flow. But this approximation is subject to correction on three scores:

1. Because the services (say) of a single machine are likely to be a large part of the total flow of machine services at a given date, application of the marginal revenue of input to the whole flow of services of the machine at that date may involve error.

1a. As a corollary to this, the revenue effect of adding a machine is likely to be less than that of subtracting one.

2. For the same reason, alteration in the number of sources owned will be most economical in association with roughly proportionate changes in use of other input: we have to deal here with complex input alterations.

3. Services of the source used at one date are likely to affect the productivity of like services at other dates, so that the terms summated are not independent.

The direction—but unfortunately not the magnitude—of the corrections needed is fairly plain. We may assume, to start with, that the marginal productivity of services used at a given date will decrease as services use expands. If so, intramarginal application of marginal revenue of input to a large increment of services will tend to overvalue additions to the stock of sources and to understate the losses from subtractions.

On the other hand, the tendency to revise other inputs parallel means a tendency to stabilize the marginal productivity of our source's services; so that the error under count 1 is seen to be less, when we allow for count 2, than might otherwise appear.

The influence of count 3 depends on the direction in which inputs of different dates affect one another. If the productivities of like input at different dates are not interrelated, there is no error; and this is a plausible assumption where the source yields services which are highly specialized. The number of hours a loom is worked on Monday will not appreciably affect the marginal productivity of a loom-hour on Tuesday. But if the source yields less specialized services (power, for instance), interrelations are probable. The extent to which the electric generator furnished power for spinning on Monday is likely to affect the productivity of power in weaving on Tuesday. We may expect like services used on different dates to reinforce rather than to weaken each other's productivity. In consequence, there is likely to be (so to speak) double counting in summating discounted marginal revenues; and the effect either of dropping or of adding a source will tend to be exaggerated by the first approximation so obtained.

All these considerations suggest that the whole shift in input associated with acquisition (as against nonacquisition) of a source must be considered as a whole. Where co-operating services are purchased as such, valuation of the source may be made residually, by deducting the sum of expense alterations for co-operating services from that of receipts alterations and discounting the residue to the present. Purchase (or production) of the source is then in order if the net value exceeds the cost—if there is what Myrdal calls an *investment gain*.[14] This reasoning, which essentially is the Marshallian doctrine of "derived demand,"[15] cannot, of course, give separate values for two or more sources whose services are to compete or to co-operate.

Commonly, the effective issue about durable sources is more narrow. It is not ordinarily so much a question *whether* to buy or

[14] G. Myrdal, *Monetary Equilibrium* (London, 1939), p. 61. Note that an "investment gain" is not an addition to net worth. It is the difference between actual net worth and net worth as it would be if the investment were arbitrarily prohibited, and is thus a part of the net worth *before* the moment for the investment arrives.

[15] A. Marshall, *Principles of Economics* (8th ed.; London, 1920), pp. 382–83 and n. 2 on p. 383.

scrap a machine (say) as *when* to replace an old machine, or *when* to add a machine of present type, or *when* to acquire one of new type. To settle this more restricted issue, it is not necessary to know the precise role and precise value of the machine in question under either of the alternative policies—only differences need be estimated. Earlier replacement, e.g., is likely to mean a different scrap (or secondhand) value for the old machine disposed of, may mean a different price for the machine bought, and will certainly change the schedule of maintenance outlays. For practical purposes, then, the difficulties of valuation of durable goods can be evaded.

If the firm has really arrived at the optimum plan, in any event, there must be no alternative scheme for dealing with durable sources which promises to increase the present discounted value of net receipts. Translating this into terms of differences between alternative schemes, there must be no possible alteration of the equilibrium plan under which the present value of the alterations in receipts, minus the present value of the alterations in outlays involved, is greater than zero.

VI. FLEXIBILITY UNDER PERFECT CERTAINTY

In actual business planning an important element is provision for flexibility. In setting out to do a particular thing in a particular way, we try to plan so that in case of need we can do it differently, or do something else. Examples of such provisions are fire insurance, maintenance of inventories, maintenance of cash balances, and use of equipment not too closely restricted to particular types of output and rates of production. This list, needless to say, is far from exhaustive.

As will appear later, the need for flexibility arises chiefly from a combination of uncertainty and capital-market imperfections. Accordingly, the issue cannot be pursued very far in the present chapter, where neither of these elements has been brought in. But even without them, flexibility has a limited role in planning; and to consider it will help put later arguments in perspective.

Some of the flexibility devices, of course, have other uses and may appear under perfect certainty without implying a desire for flexibility. The holding of inventories, for instance, may represent either the timing of operations so as to maximize profits or the reaping of discounts for bulk purchases. Insurance may be taken in the certainty that the insured property will burn. Cash balances may be held to save the costs of quick investment and disinvestment. Given subjective certainty, however, the use of these devices will be much more limited than under uncertainty. Insurance will not be held when losses are not expected; and inventories and cash balances will be so planned as to reach zero at their low ebb.

Bona fide flexibility is likely to be desirable, however, in the inner core of the firm's planning—the layout of plant. Flexibility in plant and organization means a structure which is *not* optimal for any horizontal production schedule at any level whatsoever but offers better prospects of net receipts for a prospective varying rate of output than would any structure adapted to constant output.[16]

Plainly, designing a plant ideally adapted for a horizontal production schedule involves making the fullest use of specialization. If a machine (say) is more efficient than any other at a given rate of output, it will fit into such a plant even though it may be incapable of speeding up to permit faster production and though slowing it down (or working it intermittently)may make it outrageously extravagant at a lower rate of output. But if there are

[16] Cf. the very neat formulation of the point offered by Dr. G. Stigler, "Production and Distribution in the Short Run," *Journal of Political Economy*, June, 1939, pp. 305–27: "The best technology for combining X, a fixed plant, with (say) Z units of the variable service, with a product of Y units, need not be, and for non-optimum outputs generally will not be, the same as the technology which (given the prices of the productive services) would minimize the cost of producing a product of Y. This latter technology will almost certainly require a different quantity of the fixed services. Flexibility permits this best technology for producing Y, and other non-optimum outputs, to be approximated, but at the cost of not being able to use the best-known technology for any output."

For a graphical device to describe flexibility see the discussion in terms of uncertainty, below, pp. 56–60. This analysis of flexibility under uncertainty was sketched by the writer (though diagrams and details of reasoning were omitted for lack of space) in his article in the *Quarterly Journal of Economics*, February, 1937, pp. 273–97; but for the realization that the problem is related to that of provision for fluctuations under certainty the writer is indebted to Dr. Stigler's article.

reasons for planning a varying rate of output, this inflexibility will mean a higher schedule of gross outlays when production is either above or below the scale to which the machine is adapted than would be necessary if a less specialized machine were used.

Flexibility may be achieved by cutting down services of fixed plant in proportion to services which are currently purchased, and thus more readily varied. Another device which is apparently common in real life is the use of a number of small parallel units (machines, etc.), which can be shut down or operated a few at a time, in preference to monster units.

Since we must suppose that in general entrepreneurs expect shifts in markets and therefore plan for variations in the rate of sales and purchases, they must either plan for productive flexibility or plan to take up slack by storage. Unless we are prepared to overlook perishability of goods in storage—and other storage costs—we are thus obliged to consider productive flexibility as part of planning even under certainty and smooth markets. Its importance increases vastly, of course, when market discontinuities and uncertainties are brought in.[17]

VII. REVISION OF ANTICIPATIONS AND OF PLANS

So far, the discussion of this chapter has run solely in terms of adaptations of plans to a given set of anticipations. By a slight extension of the reasoning, however, an account can readily be given of revision of plans in the light of revised estimates; and this is the task of this final section of the chapter.

For the present we need not ask *why* anticipations need be revised.[18] We shall simply suppose that a revision in estimates has happened and shall investigate the corresponding changes in plans. The general framework of the chapter, moreover, commits us to the assumption that the new expectations are held with the same feeling of certitude as the old: the entrepreneur realizes that he has erred but misses the inference that he may err again!

[17] For a fuller account of flexibility under certainty see Dr. Stigler's article referred to above.

[18] This question is best investigated after uncertainty has been brought into the discussion and is brought up for study in chap. v. below.

The simplest procedure is to consider separately the effects of revision of anticipations about selling-markets, buying-markets, and interest rates—both for short and for long stretches of future time—and conclude by considering possible complications from joint revision.

We may start with the selling-market, assuming that the revisions in estimates affect only a short interval (say a week) beginning some time in the future. It is plain at once that the primary influence of the shift will be on operations pointing toward sales of the dates in question. If, for example, the revision of estimates is pessimistic—the price expected to be realized for output sold in the interval being revised downward—a contraction of sales for that interval is indicated. This implies a contraction of scheduled output, unless the interval in question is in the very near future[19] and a corresponding contraction of input scheduled for earlier dates. This contraction will lower marginal cost of output and will raise—or at least not lower—marginal revenue of output, thus tending to restore the balance between them.

Beyond these primary effects, however, will be secondary effects resulting from interrelations of outputs and inputs of different dates. To begin with, there is an interrelation through storage of output. If markets will be worse in a certain future week, part of the goods which were to have been sold then may be marketed earlier or later, competing with goods turned out at other dates. Thus the dent in the production schedule caused by the pessimistic shift of selling-market expectations is likely to be more shallow but longer in duration than the corresponding dent in the sales schedule.

In so far as the same operations contribute both toward output of the interval in question and toward output of other intervals, a second force is brought in to prolong and make more shallow the production dent.[20] If, however, reduction of output scheduled

[19] The output of the very near future, plainly, depends chiefly on input which is past and is thus substantially determined.

[20] This joint-cost relation will both discourage output of other dates and damp the reduction for the date in question. To curtail input leading to output scheduled for the date in question will raise marginal costs for the previously scheduled levels of output at other dates. On the other hand, the necessity of carrying on certain

for this date would release important elements of input for otherwise impossible contributions toward output of other dates, the secondary effects of estimate revision on the production schedule might include upward revision of scheduled output for certain dates.

Similar considerations apply if the firm has several qualitatively different products, when selling-market estimates for one are revised. If products are "completing"—i.e., if raising scheduled production of one raises marginal productivity of input (for given rates of input) in producing the other— production schedules will tend to be revised parallel. An extreme case of this is the traditional beef-and-hides complex. If products are "competing" in production—if raising production of one lowers marginal productivities in the production of the other, or diverts resources which would have been used for the other—the revision of production schedules will tend to be inverse.

Market interdependence (either between like products of different date or between unlike products) can plainly be handled along similar lines, and no detailed analysis need be presented.

The next step is to consider revision of selling-market expectations covering a long stretch of future time. The general principles governing revision of plans are the same as in the short-interval case just discussed: there must be adjustment to a new position of maximum discounted net receipts, involving restoration of the marginal equalities discussed earlier in the chapter. But there are several points at which we must be wary in extending the results just reached.

a) While a general downward revision of (say) a schedule of selling-prices may be regarded as the sum of partial revisions in prices expected in each of a series of future weeks, the resultant revision of plans need not be the sum of the partial revisions of plans which would result from revising price expectations for the individual weeks one at a time (expectations for other weeks being unrevised). Ordinarily, the total effect will be more drastic than the sum of the partial effects. If we think again of a pessimistic (downward) shift of selling-price expectations, maintaining pro-

---

operations for the benefit of output of other dates will make marginal cost fall rapidly as output scheduled for the date in question is cut. Where outputs of different dates are strongly "completing" in production, therefore, the output dent will be shallowed and prolonged.

duction for a particular week is no longer made attractive by the prospect of shifting part of this output to sales at other dates. Furthermore, a general downward revision of the production schedule permits cutting out purchases of equipment, etc., which could not be dispensed with merely by revision for a particular week.

b) A general revision may make the difference between staying in business and liquidating; a partial revision is very unlikely to do so.

c) If the general revision affects selling-markets of all dates following one in the near future (even though the worsening, as against previous estimates, is the same for all dates), the divergence of the revised from the original production schedule is likely to be gradual. This results from the fact already cited[21] that the input associated with any particular item of output is chiefly of earlier date than that output. Accordingly, most of the decisions affecting output of next week (say) have already been taken; and those decisions have largely predetermined those which are still to be made about that output; whereas decisions for output of a year hence are much more free. To cut next week's output 50 per cent below that scheduled may save only 5 per cent of the selling-value of the output to be sacrificed; while a 50 per cent increase of next week's scheduled output may involve crushing expenses. Similar shifts in next year's scheduled output are likely to be at more reasonable cost. "Haste makes waste," says the proverb: sharp revision of production and input schedules for the very near future is rarely profitable.

If the revision of anticipations applies to buying-markets, the effects are similar. A pessimistic (upward) revision of estimates for the price of a material in a short future interval, e.g., will discourage use of that material at that date, and also use of co-operating input at other dates. If (as is plausible) substitute inputs are available, their use will be encouraged.

The effect of changes in buying-market anticipations upon output is likely to be diffused over time even though it relates only to buying-prices of a short interval. As with revision of selling-

[21] Cf. pp. 19–20 above.

market estimates, the presumption holds that the effect upon plans of a revision of estimates covering a long period will exceed the sum of the effects of small partial revisions which in some would amount to the estimate revision in question.

A change in expectations about interest rates will change the present discounted values of all receipts and outlays scheduled under the existing plans for dates beyond that where the new interest-rate schedule begins to diverge from previous expectations. This will involve relative shifts in discounted marginal revenues and corresponding discounted marginal costs, and hence readjustment of plans to restore balance.

Of special interest is the reaction if the whole schedule of expected future rates, from the present onward, is revised uniformly (being written down, say, by 1 per cent per annum).[22] This means that all marginal revenues gain in discounted value, those for input of long reaction interval[23] most strongly. The consequence, plainly, will be an expansion of scheduled input—particularly in operations for the distant future, to restore equality (on a discounted basis) between marginal costs and marginal revenues.

In planning future output, however, it is necessary to allow for the effect of a higher schedule of present input of long reaction interval in raising the productivity of future co-operating input of short reaction interval. Input schedules of the first sort (long reaction interval) will be revised sharply upward beginning with dates in the very near future; whereas input schedules of the second sort will also be revised upward but will diverge only very gradually—as the effect of increases in earlier co-operating input takes hold—from the schedules previously planned.

This last effect of lower interest—first a stimulation of input of long reaction interval, later a stimulation of input of shorter reaction interval—has some affinity with the Hayekian doctrine of the role of interest in the business cycle. In fact, the writer was first put on the track of it by Dr. Hayek's influence. But the reader should note that the effect here described is entirely within the planning of a single firm. To project such reasoning to inter-firm relations involves making assumptions about the compatibility or in-

[22] See the very interesting treatment of the question in Hicks, *Value and Capital*, pp. 216 ff., which goes much further than the account here offered.

[23] Cf. above, p. 19.

compatibility of various entrepreneurs' plans and estimates. This is beyond the scope of the present essay; and in fact the writer doubts the significance of such interfirm extensions under any conditions.

Since it will give inducements for an immediate expansion of input and purchases, while the resulting expansion of production, sales, and receipts is not immediately effective, the optimistic (downward) revision of interest expectations will make it worth the firm's while to take in more outside capital—just the traditional effect of lowered interest.

The same will be true, however, of optimistic revisions of buying-price or of selling-price expectations. In general, the financial effects of the shift of operating plans resulting from any sort of revision of estimates are bound to appear more promptly on the outlay side than on the receipts side, unless there happens to be a compensating shift in inventories. This parallelism between interest revisions and price-expectation revisions is merely an illustration of the general principle that any part of a firm's plan may be affected by a revision of any part of its system of estimates of the future.

The reader will note that no attempt has been made to cover the effect of revision of engineering estimates. In this field, almost anything may happen. Two principles however, may be serviceable later: (1) such revision is likely to favor greater output and (2), as with price-expectation revision, and for the same reason, divergence of revised from previous schedules will gather momentum slowly.

CHAPTER III

BUSINESS PLANNING UNDER RATIONING AND PRICE-FIXING

I. THE PROBLEM OF MARKET DISCONTINUITIES

IN THE preceding chapters the firm has been assumed free to buy all it chooses, sell all it chooses, offer to deal at any prices it chooses. The only limitation upon operations has been taken to lie in considerations of profitability, in the light of technology, existing facilities, and prices. On the side of capital financing also, the only limitation has been taken to be profitability in the light of open-market interest rates.

All these assumptions do some violence to facts. Many firms sell or buy subject to external price regulation (think of utility rate fixation and minimum-wage determination). To some extent in peacetime and very widely in wartime, direct restrictions on the volume of purchases or sales (rationing restrictions) limit operations. The assumption of a free capital market, finally, is desperately unrealistic; as will be shown presently, capital-rationing is an essential trait of the capitalist economy. Capital-rationing will be the chief topic of this chapter; but commodity-rationing and price-fixing afford a natural introduction to this main problem and have been so little explored as to have some independent interest.

Price-fixing will be said to take place when some force external to the firm fixes upper or lower limits to the prices at which the firm is allowed to buy or sell; and it is *effective* when it leads the firm to deal at prices other than those it would make in the absence of innovation. We are primarily interested in price-fixing applied to firms which have some monopoly power (or are subject to rationing); for so long as a firm is free to buy or sell unlimited quantities at a price externally fixed, its reaction will be the same as if it were governed by a perfectly competitive market.

Rationing will be said to exist when the firm is in some way prevented from buying, selling, or borrowing unlimited amounts at the prices and interest rates in effect. It is effective when the limits set fall short of the volume of dealings the firm would choose to carry on if free.

The common element in the problems of rationing and price-fixing is that both involve discontinuities in market conditions. In the case of sales-rationing, e.g., once the limit of permitted sales is reached, the firm has no use for additional output, and marginal revenue of output drops to zero. Production will go no further, however low marginal costs.[1] Or if purchases rather than sales are rationed, arriving at the limit means the end of possibilities of raising output by expanding the type of input in question: in effect, marginal cost of output becomes infinite. The effect of rationing, therefore, is to make valuation by marginal cost or marginal revenue indeterminate.[2]

The discontinuities of price-fixing are very similar. If, e.g., a monopolist is subjected to a maximum selling-price, his marginal revenue of output for any scale of output up to the largest salable at that price will equal the maximum price. To sell more, the price must be lowered, and marginal revenue of output will drop suddenly to a much lower level. Parallel arguments apply to the fixation of minimum buying-prices. As we shall see, price-fixing may either stimulate or retard activity;[3] whereas rationing is bound to retard it.

The effects of rationing and price-fixing being so closely allied, it is simplest to divide the material of this chapter according to the parts of the firm's operations directly affected by the restriction

[1] Precisely this problem was briefly considered by Cournot (*Mathematical Principles of the Theory of Wealth*, trans. N. Bacon [New York, 1929], p. 58); and he also reached the conclusion that further output will have no value to the firm and that cost will lose its normal role in governing production.

[2] The principles involved are the same if there is a market with "steps": if, e.g., purchases may be pushed beyond a certain limit only on penalty of an extra charge for each additional unit. "Stepped" markets will be of considerable interest in this chapter, especially in connection with capital problems.

[3] See the discussion by Mrs. Robinson, *Economics of Imperfect Competition* (London, 1933), pp. 163 and 295, and the illustrative diagrams (showing the discontinuities), *ibid.*, pp. 161–62, 294.

rather than according to type of restriction. Successive sections, therefore, will deal in turn with selling-markets, buying-markets, and capital-market restrictions.

II. SELLING-PRICE REGULATION AND SALES-RATIONING

Even in ordinary times many firms are subject to control of their selling-prices through government agencies. Maximums are commonly fixed for electric power and gas, railway transportation, etc. Minimums (as for taxicab rides and bituminous coal) are not very rare. In wartime the number of price controls (particularly maximums) expands.

Fixing a maximum selling-price, if it is effective (i.e., if the firm does not find it worth while to sell on so large a scale as to push the price below the allowed maximum), simulates the effect of rendering competition perfect. In the absence of such a restriction, the firm's marginal revenue of output would be less than the selling-price, since selling more output would involve cutting the price on the previous sales volume. But if the firm cannot in any case exceed the maximum fixed, expansion of sales does not necessitate price reduction, and marginal revenue of output becomes identical with selling-price. So long as the maximum is low enough to be effective, yet higher than the marginal revenue of output at which the firm would operate if there were no price control, the effect is to stimulate output.[4]

A reduction of the maximum selling-price below the marginal revenue or output which would otherwise have existed will reduce the maximum-profit volume of output. If (as sometimes happens) the firm is required to sell to all comers at or below the maximum price, it may possibly find its sales volume unprofitably large; but this case is of small practical importance.

Fixing a minimum price, if effective, forces the firm to charge more—and therefore to sell less—than if it were unrestricted. The firm's sales schedule will be limited to that obtainable while

[4] Cf. *ibid.*, pp. 159–63. It is readily shown that the percentage by which price can be lowered without reducing output is given by the reciprocal of the elasticity of demand. In a "timeless" case, let sales be x and the selling-price y. Then the elasticity of demand $E = (-y/x)(dx/dy)$, and the marginal revenue of output, which we may call $R = d(xy)/dx = x(dy/dx) + y$. Substituting, we have $R = y(1 - 1/E)$.

charging the minimum allowed. The only difference of this situation from sales-rationing (where a sales schedule is fixed from outside) is that under minimum selling-price fixation the sales schedule may be expanded by sales promotion.

Sales-rationing may be said to occur whenever some sales schedule of a firm is given a maximum lying below the schedule the firm would lay out if unregulated. Something of the sort is an indispensable weapon for any monopolistic combination of independent firms, in order to make price-cutting unprofitable; the "sales quota" is a standard device for governing cartels.[5]

Under sales-rationing the firm's market expectations must be thought of as consisting of a rationing-allowance schedule (or quota) and a rationing-price schedule, the latter representing the prices expected to rule for output.[6] At dates when rationing is effective, an increase of output—since it cannot be sold—brings no increase of revenue. Marginal revenue of output thus drops to zero and affords no guide for internal valuations of output. For such dates, however, a marginal cost of output can in general be calculated, and a supply-price schedule worked out—the price at each date representing the cost at which a unit could be replaced if (say) accidentally destroyed.

So long as the rationing-price schedule nowhere falls below the schedule of supply prices, there is no question of selling less than the quota. This implies a certain insensitivity of the plan to changes in anticipations. A change in the expected rationing-price schedule, so long as it involves no reduction below supply price for any date, will leave the entire production plan unaffected. A change in estimated costs altering the supply-price schedule, so long as it involves no increase above the rationing-price for any date, will leave the production schedule unaffected; though it may of course affect the composition of input and the plans for sales of types of output not rationed. The firm's net

[5] In some cartels a member can exceed his sales quota subject to fine, giving a "stepped market" on which marginal revenue of output for the member firm drops at the quota level from the cartel's selling-price to price *less* fine.

[6] It is possible that a higher price can be obtained by selling (at some dates) less than the quota. This possibility is here ignored, to simplify the forms of words used in the text. It makes little logical difference.

worth, plainly, will be less under rationing than if sales were un-restricted.

Sales-rationing commonly exists when there is price-fixing. During the war of 1914–18 it was coupled with maximum-price fixation; and under cartel schemes it goes with minimum-price fixation. Given the rationing allowance, however, it matters very little for the firm's policy whether the selling-price is fixed by a free market or by a dominant authority, unless evasion of the rationing restriction is contemplated.

III. BUYING-PRICE REGULATION AND INPUT-RATIONING

Price-fixing applied to input is not uncommon. An important example which lies ready to hand is fixation of minimum wages. Maximum buying-prices obviously exist for all firms whose monopolistic suppliers—like electric-power companies and railways —are subject to maximum selling-prices. More rarely, they apply to buyers whose suppliers have no monopoly position, as in the case of the maximum wages long fixed by English justices of the peace.

An effective minimum buying-price—like an effective maximum selling-price—simulates the effect of perfect competition.[7] While raising the average cost of input for any volume of purchases short of that for which the price fixed is the supply price, it will lower the marginal cost through much of that range. So long as the minimum is lower than the marginal cost of input which would have been effective in the absence of regulation, it will stimulate rather than inhibit use of the input in question.[8] Whether or not it exceeds this figure, an effective minimum will of course impair the firm's profit prospects.

Fixing a minimum buying-price for one input will of course

[7] This assumes that competition with other buyers was not perfect before the price was fixed. If it was, the analysis of the firm is not affected by price-fixing. To the firm in such a situation, imposition of an effective minimum price is equivalent to an unfavorable turn of the competitive buying market. Viewing the market as a whole, there will presumably be an unmarketable excess supply of the input; but this is not our concern here.

[8] See the symmetrical discussion of maximum selling-prices above, p. 35; see also Mrs. Robinson, *op. cit.*, pp. 294–95.

affect the firm's demand for others. Use of complementary inputs will move in the same direction, use of substitutes in the opposite direction. Since complementarity among inputs is the rule,[9] output will move in the same direction as the input directly affected, though probably not so sharply.

Input-rationing is defined as the fixation of a maximum permitted purchase schedule for something the firm buys,[10] which may not be exceeded however much the entrepreneur may wish to do so. It may arise "naturally" if the firm is a buying monopoly and is able to sweep the market of all available supplies without paying the full demand price for these supplies.[11] It may arise through outside fixation of a maximum buying-price, if the total supply available at that price is inadequate.[12] It may arise from wartime restrictions on the use of labor, transport, and strategic materials. In peacetime it may spring from the necessity of apportioning import quotas, or may be an expedient of dealers who have a temporary shortage and prefer to ration customers rather than lose good-will by raising prices sharply. Incidentally, there is also an interesting class of rationed free goods: diversion of water for power and irrigation, parking-space in city streets, etc.

By symmetry with the selling-market, it is plain that a firm subject to input-rationing will anticipate a rationing-allowance (maximum permitted purchase schedule) and rationing-price schedule. In the circumstances, however, it will not be able to lay out a schedule of marginal costs of input, since no amount of extra outlay will increase the available flow. Input, therefore, can be valued only by its marginal revenue.

By symmetry with the selling-market situations already

---

[9] Cf. J. R. Hicks, *Value and Capital* (Oxford, 1939), p. 95.

[10] Note that this is in the first instance *purchase-rationing*. The argument of the text, assuming that restriction of purchases is identical with restriction of input, is admittedly oversimplified. But the verbal complications resulting from explicit allowance for possible divergence of input from purchases (through storage or purchase of durable sources) are enormous, and the gain in generality small; the correction, accordingly, is left to the reader.

[11] Think, e.g., of a small-town factory, or of the Standard Oil in the days when it was the only major buyer in the Pennsylvania fields.

[12] Cf. the discussion of minimum selling-price as sales-rationing, above, pp. 35–36.

analyzed, we may think of the entrepreneur as setting up a schedule of demand prices (i.e., discounted marginal revenues) for input, assuming the full allowance to be used. So long as this schedule lies throughout its length above the schedule of rationing-prices (or above zero if the rationed input is free), the full rationing-allowance will be used. As with the selling-market, revisions of price expectations which do not make the two price schedules cross will leave the input schedule unaffected.

These propositions are subject to two qualifications. In the first place, rationing may be *directly* effective through only part of the firm's plan, the input scheduled for other dates lying below the rationing-allowance. Even for those dates, however, rationing may be *indirectly* effective. For the level of input of this type which the firm can employ at a given level of discounted marginal revenue of input may be limited by restrictions on co-operating input of earlier or later dates.

In the second place, the fact that changes in the schedule of rationing-prices will affect profit prospects means that it may possibly push the entrepreneur over a margin of doubt as to whether to go out of business. Lowering the rationing-price may lead to survival, raising it to extinction. In this event, the effect on operations will of course be drastic. Similar considerations apply to sales-rationing.

The effect of rationing in making business plans insensitive to changes in price anticipations will of course be intensified if rationing impinges upon the firm at several points. If several types of inputs—or some inputs and some outputs—are rationed, the production plan may be almost completely rigid in the face of changes below a certain threshold, beyond which the effectiveness of rationing is destroyed by unfavorable price shifts.

IV. CAPITAL-RATIONING

Capital-rationing will be said to occur when the amount of capital financing a firm obtains is limited otherwise than by considerations of profitability in the light of buying-markets, selling-markets, and the interest rate charged.[13] This situation—the chief object of study in the present chapter—is normal for the greater part of the firms in the real world, though perhaps less

[13] Note that input-rationing and sales-rationing may occur without capital-rationing; though the latter may for some purposes be regarded as a sort of generalized input-rationing.

common among large than among small firms. In fact, as was hinted at the beginning of this chapter, widespread capital-rationing is an institutional necessity of capitalism.

This necessity may be made clear simply by specifying the meaning of a free capital market. A firm not subject to capital-rationing, and thus enjoying a free market, must be free to draw in as much in the way of outside capital funds as the entrepreneur thinks profitable. It must be able to obtain funds, moreover, in equity form or by borrowing, and, if the latter, through borrowing at any maturity the entrepreneur chooses.

Investors, plainly, can give such scope only to entrepreneurs in whose good faith and good judgment they feel implicit confidence. Since some would-be borrowers intend to abscond with the borrowed funds, others hope to use fresh capital to stave off a day of reckoning, and even borrowers in good faith often grossly overestimate their business prospects—and particularly since the investor has no infallible way of identifying such bad credit risks—most borrowers must expect to be regarded with some suspicion.

It will be observed that this explanation clearly shows capital-rationing to be an effect of uncertainty. The institutions of the capital market, discussed below, would be different if uncertainty did not exist.

Accordingly, it may seem inappropriate to deal with rationing of capital under assumptions of perfect certainty, as is done in this chapter. What justifies this procedure is the fact that it is uncertainty in the estimates of outsiders—not in the entrepreneur's own thinking—which determines the firm's relation to the capital market. In principle we might classify problems of the firm as follows: (a) entrepreneur's estimates certain, in an environment where all others also feel certainty; (b) entrepreneur's estimates uncertain, in a world of certainty; (c) entrepreneur's estimates certain, in an environment where others are uncertain; and (d) entrepreneur's estimates as well as those of others uncertain. It might appear that we were under obligation to analyze these cases in order. But upon inspection it appears that case (b) is trivial. Case (d) is our real focus of interest. Case (c) is a useful approximation from which (d) can be developed. Case (a) has already been examined in chapter ii, so far as it is needed. The distinctive traits of case (c) are brought in in the present chapter.

The institutions of the capital market are deeply affected by the investor's uncertainty. To see how this leads to capital-rationing, however, it is necessary to start with a classification of possible sources of capital funds for a firm, namely: (i) the capitalist-entrepreneur himself, either "plowing in" part of the firm's earnings or investing funds drawn from his outside income or other assets (i.e., accepting a negative withdrawal schedule); (ii) "outsiders" buying participations in the equity (i.e., taking partnerships or buying new stock issues but not gaining a voice in the firm's policy decisions); (iii) "outsiders" making loans to the firm; and (iv) owners of durable sources of services, providing capital by leasing land or buildings or by renting machines to the firm. The degree of flexibility of each of these sources must be studied.

Entrepreneurial investment is always somewhat flexible. But unless the person (or group) controlling the firm has large outside resources, this flexibility has limits, set by income and outside capital assets.

The second source—"outside" equity participations—has more complex limits. Ordinarily a certain amount of funds can be had from friends of the controlling group, on terms which amount to inactive partnership. This sort of financing differs only in degree from entrepreneurial investment. To go further with equity financing, stock must be publicly floated. Here limits are determined largely by investment-banking practices. In some cases no stock at all can be sold, for lack of an investment-banking sponsor. When sales are possible, it is commonly necessary to float stock in large blocks. In any event, the amount of outside capital which can be drawn in without the original owners surrendering control —except when investors are in a state of such high elation that they will buy nonvoting common shares—is limited by the size of the "insider" equity. This limitation is of course the reason why the very success of a firm sometimes costs the owners their control: they may uncover a business opportunity which is worth more to the possessors of large capitals than to themselves.

The third source—borrowing—also presents limitations. In our kind of world the savers who provide capital are themselves not competent judges of the competence and honesty of businessmen wanting capital. This fact leads lenders to take refuge in the requirement of security—which is more easily judged—or in the employment of such investment middlemen as bankers, trust companies, investment bankers, insurance companies, and mortgage lending agencies. These middlemen in their turn commonly exact security. This is partly to engender confidence in the ultimate investor—who has learned to his cost that dealing with investment middlemen may be every bit as dangerous as direct dealing with borrowers—and partly to eliminate the need of expensive investigations. Hence investment specialists (in part under the influence of laws governing trusteeship) have built up systems of more or less arbitrary rules, which are followed also by many private investors. Under these rules, borrowing power depends on the existence in the business—or acquisition by it—of certain types of inventory items, or of real estate not otherwise pledged. Commonly it depends also on the maintenance of a certain ratio of cash assets to current liabilities and of equity to total liabilities.

The fourth source of capital—renting of capital goods—strikes the writer as of secondary importance and is mentioned chiefly for the sake of formal completeness. Given a free capital market, the existence of this source would make no difference whatsoever: there would be next to no difference between (say) hiring a machine and borrowing funds to buy it.

For firms of very poor credit standing in a world where investors feel uncertainty, the institution of rental makes a real difference. Owners of property—especially of highly durable and immovable property such as land and buildings, but also of machinery—are legally much better protected if they hire out their property than if they sell it and lend the price on mortgage. Consequently they can afford to rent to firms whose credit standing would not permit buying.

Rental, however, cannot provide all that a firm needs; and for firms of good credit standing the costs of administration of rental make it better to buy. This source of capital, therefore, is on the whole to be regarded merely as a secondary mitigation of capital-rationing and will not be systematically considered in the discussion which follows.

From these considerations about the nature of the capital market we may draw a chain of consequences: (i) the average interest rate paid by a firm will rise as its debts (or outside equity) become larger relative to the inside equity; (ii) ordinarily there will be discrimination between different types of financing, and this rise of rates will express itself in a stepped market; (iii) ordinarily this will mean capital-rationing; and (iv) the rates on interest appropriate for the firm's internal calculations will in general be higher than the highest rate paid. The development of these consequences will reveal the effect of capital-rationing upon business planning. Certain further consequences will be reserved for discussion in the final section of this chapter.

If investors providing capital for a firm normally based their decisions on study of the would-be borrower's character and prospects, we might expect to find a smooth rise in interest rates as the borrower's debt rose in proportion to his own equity. This expectation arises from the basic assumption that the investor is uncertain about the businessman's intention and ability to repay. As the equity thins out, both the temptation upon the entrepreneur to deceive his creditors and the likelihood of his being forced into insolvency by some adverse turn of markets will become stronger. The return which the investor will receive if all goes well must thus be placed higher to compensate for the increasing probability that all will not go well and the investor will receive less.

From the investor's point of view, this insistence on a higher nominal rate as the equity grows thinner represents "compensation for risk." From the borrower's point of view—since part of the "risk" turns on his own dishonesty and part on uncertainty about his business prospects which he is assumed not to share—all charges incurred by borrowing are homogeneous. But if the rate rises as borrowings increase, by the analogy of price theory, we must distinguish a marginal cost of outside funds[14] higher than the interest rate paid. This marginal cost then becomes the rate appropriate for calculations within the firm.[15]

In the real world, however, investigations of borrowers are too costly and difficult to be thoroughly made. The investment rules of thumb which fill the place of investigation are so framed that a

[14] To take an example in finite increments, suppose the firm owes $100,000, subject to interest at 5 per cent. If it can increase its debt to $110,000 only by paying 5½ per cent on the whole debt, such an increase will raise interest charges by $775 per annum, or at the rate of 7¾ per cent on the increment of debt.

[15] Plainly this means that the firm's own policy will affect the interest rates used for discounting; and in consequence difficulties arise as to what the entrepreneur maximizes. For a proposed solution see Appen. pp. 92–95 below.

smooth rise of interest rates with a thinning of the equity is un-likely. Instead, the firm is confronted with a series of opportu-nities for raising funds, each with its own interest rate and its own rules, and each—ordinarily—having fairly definite quantitative limits. That is, the entrepreneur obtains capital on a "stepped" market.

A firm can borrow (say) a certain amount secured by inven-tories and receivables at a low rate, more secured by a first mort-gage on land and buildings at a higher rate, still more on second mortgage or debentures at a still higher rate; possibly it can float preferred shares at a rate slightly below or slightly above that on debentures. Sometimes expansion of borrowing on one of these steps entails a rise of the rate charged. But it is a fair working approximation to think of each as offering an interest rate which varies little with the amount taken, while granting access at that rate to a definite maximum sum.

In these circumstances, if the firm uses only part of its allot-ment on a given step of the market, the rate effective on that step will be to the firm much like an open-market competitive rate.[16] If it uses all that is available on one step, but cannot afford the rate at the next step (or has access to no higher step), it is subject to rationing, and the rate loses meaning.

Before proceeding to the determination of the rate under rationing, we may well consider the peculiar results of an incidental effect of the investor's arbitrary attitude, namely, the *maturity restriction*. This means the attempt of lenders to protect themselves by trying to limit the borrower to certain uses of their funds, expressed through requirements of collateral. Typically, collateral found desirable is of one of two extreme types. At one end of the scale we find goods easy to liquidate (inventory, receivables, goods in process) and at the other goods durable and hard to make off with (land and build-ings); intermediate types are not favored.

A borrower on short term is commonly required to invest the loan pro-ceeds in "liquid" assets—perhaps even in a specified bill of goods. But the economist will realize that the lender's criterion as to how the loan is used—namely, the character of the next transaction after borrowing—is artificial. If any particular transaction is related to the loan, it is that which must have been foregone if the loan had been refused. Inasmuch as materials,

---

[16] The firm's plans may involve shifting from one step to another in future, in which case the interest schedule applied in its calculations will jump sharply at that date.

labor, etc., are indispensable, this marginal transaction is likely to be some outlay for purchase or maintenance of fixed capital.[17] So long as the firm has unused borrowing power on the short-term step, in consequence of holding unpledged assets of suitable character, it may be able to make the short-term rate effective for all its purposes. But if it can increase such borrowings only by acquiring more suitable assets, the discrimination will be effective. In this case the firm may actually have to apply a higher interest rate to calculations about other purchases than those short-term borrowing will finance, and multiple internal rates of interest will exist.

Similar considerations apply to long-term loans and their associated specialized collateral. If the firm holds unmortgaged real estate, it can "divert" long-term borrowings to any use it chooses. But if it can borrow more only by acquiring more such goods, the maturity restriction will warp its plan in favor of such purchases, and multiple internal rates will exist.

The multiple-rate phenomenon simply reflects the influence of a special-purpose subsidy. Analogous differentials in the valuation of (say) raw cotton might exist if the government would pay a subsidy of 5 cents per pound for cotton used in making colored goods but not for cotton used in making white goods.

Under capital-rationing, as under commodity-rationing, the entrepreneur's estimates must be taken to include a rationing-allowance schedule and rationing-price schedule. The former, in this case, will be a schedule of maximum amounts of outside funds which the firm expects to be allowed to hold at various future dates; the latter will be a schedule of interest rates expected to figure in actual contracts. Rationing will be said to be directly effective for intervals when the firm plans to use all the outside funds permitted.

For such intervals—as can be seen by direct analogy with commodity-rationing—the firm would be willing to borrow its full allowance even though forced to pay more than the rationing-rate of interest. For intervals when part of the firm's allowance is to be unused, the anticipated rationing-rate will be the immediate limitation. But rationing will still be indirectly effective if inability to finance certain later transactions limits earlier investment opportunities, as ordinarily it must.

The rate of interest which should be used for discounting across

[17] Strictly, the incidence of the loss of borrowing power would be spread over all lines of purchasing; but the elasticity of purchases linked with output of the very near future is bound to be lower than that of purchases aiming toward distant effects.

intervals when rationing will not be directly effective is plainly the rationing-rate, for intervals of direct effectiveness some higher rate. But to derive a schedule of internal rates of interest (corresponding to the demand-price schedules and supply-price schedules of earlier sections) is a difficult task.

For a real determination, we must appeal to the forces which Irving Fisher calls "impatience" and "investment opportunity."[18] To begin with, we may confine ourselves temporarily to the investment opportunity side by assuming that for several years ahead capital-rationing is to be directly effective and absolute: even the capitalist-entrepreneur himself will make a rigidly predetermined contribution to the firm's capital. For the next few years,[19] then, the withdrawal schedule is fixed, and no funds can be borrowed.

Under these assumptions we may arrive at a schedule of internal rates by starting from the rationing-rate schedule and making corrections, guiding ourselves by the rule that for each item of scheduled input there should be balance between the present discounted values of marginal cost and marginal revenue of input.

If valuations are correct, it is plain that a dollar's worth of input at a given date must not have a higher marginal revenue than another dollar's worth. For input of given date, discounted marginal revenues of input must be proportionate to marginal costs of input. But by hypothesis, since capital-rationing is effective, the firm cannot borrow as much as it would like. Hence its disbursements are lower than it would like, and input must be too small to bring discounted marginal revenue and marginal cost to equality. Taking the borrowing-rate as valuation criterion, it is plain that discounted marginal revenues will exceed marginal

---

[18] *Theory of Interest* (New York, 1930), *passim*. The "internal rate" of this essay corresponds to Fisher's "marginal rate of return over cost" (see *ibid.*, pp. 159–61).

[19] The withdrawal schedule of course embodies the planned contribution (positive or negative) of the entrepreneur to his firm's capital funds. We cannot assume it fixed for the life of the firm, however, without abolishing our problem; for this would fix the firm's net worth regardless of the decisions under study. Hence our compromise. We should think of the withdrawal schedule as fixed for a period extending so far into the future that productivities of current input will not be appreciably affected by alterations of input scheduled for dates after the end of the period.

costs. By our rule of proportionality, this excess should be by a uniform percentage, which we may christen *surplus value* (not in the Marxian sense).

It is readily demonstrated, however, that the rule of uniform surplus value does not lead to maximum gain. For if part of the firm's expenditure were shifted from input affecting distant output to input affecting output of the near future—from uses of long to uses of short reaction interval—the firm's output and receipts in the near future would grow. This would permit increased outlays then, enabling the firm to reap two surplus values instead of one. It follows that under the optimum plan (by the criterion of discounted values calculated at rationing-rates) surplus value must be greater for input of long than for input of short reaction interval.

This may be illustrated arithmetically as follows. Suppose the rationing-rate for two years ahead will be 5 per cent, and the firm has worked out a provisional plan offering 10 per cent surplus value for input of every date. Then an increment of present input worth $1.00 must have an undiscounted marginal revenue of input under the plan of $(1.00) (1.10) (1.05) when used in an operation with a reaction interval of one year, and of $(1.00) (1.10) (1.05) (1.05) in an operation with a reaction interval of two years. The first gives $1.155 at the end of Year 1, the second $1.213 at the end of Year 2. But by hypothesis, reinvesting our $1.155 at the end of year 1 will yield $(1.155) (1.10) (1.05) or $1.334 at the end of Year 2. The firm would thus gain about $0.121 (in dollars of Year 2) by transferring a dollar of expenditure to input bearing fruit in one year. This transfer, however, would raise the surplus value of two-year input and lower that of one-year input.

To readjust the distribution of expenditure so as to reapportion surplus value in this fashion comes to the same thing as to charge higher interest. As a second approximation to the optimum plan, then, we may imagine the entrepreneur discounting by a schedule of interest rates above the borrowing rates and again distributing surplus value uniformly over all inputs. The resulting percentage of surplus value will of course be less. But a further improvement could be made by readjusting input again, so as to raise surplus value on input of long reaction interval.[20] Again, such a readjust-

[20] If surplus value were 5 per cent, interest 9 per cent, under the second approximation, the one-year investment of $1.00 would yield $1.1445, and this amount reinvested would yield $1.3098 at the end of Year 2. The direct two-year investment of $1.00 would yield $1.2473 at Year 2, leaving a difference of $0.0625.

ment can be made by reckoning at higher rates. But so long as surplus value is there to be reapportioned, realignment to a still higher interest schedule will be advantageous. The plan will not reach final adjustment until the schedule of rates used for discounting will just eliminate surplus value for all dates.

The internal-rate schedule is thus a characteristic of the optimum business plan. An average "rate of return over cost" can be ascertained by purely arithmetical operations for any business plan whatsoever.[21] But a schedule of internal rates cannot be worked out from any plan which lacks a highly specific form of internal consistency. If we simply selected at random one of the list of plans permitted by technology, we should find that a schedule of rates which equalized marginal cost and discounted marginal revenue for some inputs would leave discrepancies for other inputs. A "marginal productivity of capital"—like a marginal productivity for anything having alternative uses—can be spoken of only when the advantages of all alternatives are in balance.

We are now ready to release the entrepreneur's withdrawal schedule from its hypothetical fixity. If for any date, under the plan just determined, his personal time-preference rate would exceed the firm's internal rate, the withdrawal schedule would rise, and funds would be diverted from the firm to the entrepreneur's personal use. But this again would restrict the firm's power to buy input, creating a surplus value to be apportioned. Accordingly, a plan leading to a schedule of internal rates below the entrepreneur's personal schedule of time-preference rates would not be optimal. It would be adjusted toward a higher internal-rate schedule and higher withdrawal schedule.

Reciprocally, if the provisional plan yielded a schedule of internal rates above the entrepreneur's personal rates, adjustment would involve reduction of scheduled withdrawals for the near future. Input would expand, and the elimination of negative surplus value would yield a lower internal-rate schedule. Equilibrium in planning thus involves mutual adjustment of the firm and the entrepreneur's household, to give like internal-rate schedules in both.

---

[21] See Fisher, *op. cit.*, pp. 155–58, and K. E. Boulding, "Theory of a Single Investment," *Quarterly Journal of Economics*, Vol. XLIX, No. 3 (May, 1935).

Since the rate charged by the entrepreneur (as householder) to himself (as manager of the firm) will rise as the amount he invests in the firm rises, it may appear that the solution should equalize the marginal cost of capital (more than the time-preference rate) with the marginal return on capital, along the lines of the theory of monopoly.

This solution, however, is specious. In the first place, the internal rate (as defined) is already marginal to the firm. In the second place, the time-preference rate is already marginal to the household. To reckon with the marginal cost to the firm of the entrepreneur's own funds is to imagine him in his business capacity "monopolistically exploiting" himself in his personal capacity, which is fantastic. The complex of household and firm must here be considered jointly.

Contrary to the position with input- and sales- rationing, the schedule of internal rates is not a precise equivalent for the schedule of anticipated open-market opportunities which would lead to the formulation of the same business plan. The reason is that the rationing-rates of interest themselves affect the intensity of capital-rationing. If rationing-rates are reduced, the firm has more funds available to buy input or finance withdrawals, and its schedule of internal rates will be slightly lowered. Raising ration-rates toward the schedule of internal rates, on the other hand, would raise the latter.

Like other types of rationing, capital-rationing tends to make the business plan less sensitive to moderate shifts in marketing anticipations. But since capital-rationing is less of a barrier to substitution than input-rationing or sales-rationing, its effect in stabilizing particular input schedules and production schedules will be less substantial. It is chiefly changes in rationing-rates of interest which are cut off from affecting plans; and even here, as was argued in the last paragraph, some attenuated influence will be felt.

V. RAMIFICATIONS OF CAPITAL-RATIONING

Coexistence of capital-rationing with other types of rationing has certain peculiarities which need discussion. In the first place, changes in rationing-prices of input and output, when capital-rationing is in force, will alter its intensity. A fall of the rationing-price on a rationed input item, or a rise of the rationing-price for rationed sales, increases the firm's ability to buy physical input and thus amounts to a relaxation of capital-rationing. The contrary applies to opposite price changes.

In terms of effects both upon valuations within the firm and upon plans for operations, reduction in the expected scale of any rationing-allowance acts much like unfavorable revision of anticipations for prices or interest rates under free markets. The forces on the market which tend to bring about tightening of commodity-rationing, moreover, are of much the same character as those bringing on unfavorable price changes. Accordingly, the lack of attention to rationing in business-cycle theory is unlikely to involve even qualitative error on the commodity side.

On the capital-market side, however, it appears that the forces which lower open-market interest rates also tend to tighten capital-rationing for firms in weak condition.[22] The consideration of capital-rationing may thus affect our views on the hypothesis that capital-market changes on the downswing prepare the ground for recovery. The chief importance of rationing in the context of business fluctuations, however, is as a factor affecting reactions to uncertainty. This will be made clear in the next chapter.

The existence of capital-market imperfections, reflecting uncertainty on the part of "outsiders," gives the firm's management inducements to modify plans in the direction of respectability, with a view to enlarging the rationing-allowance. Putting part of earning assets into apparently unremunerative "liquid" form may pay for itself by increasing borrowing power (enabling the firm to acquire more earning assets) or by reducing rationing-rates by putting the firm on a more favorable market "step." Similar benefits may flow from outlays to pay for insurance; ability to borrow on mortgage, e.g., depends on taking out fire insurance. These considerations further reinforce the argument of the last chapter[23] that measures looking toward flexibility may be rational even though the entrepreneur feels no uncertainty.

[22] Cf. C. O. Hardy and J. Viner, *Report of the Availability of Bank Credit in the Seventh Federal Reserve District* (Washington, 1935). It appears that on the downswing interest rates for "eligible" borrowers drop, but that many firms experience sharp reduction of their lines of credit and new firms find credit hard to establish.

[23] See above, pp. 25–27.

CHAPTER IV

THE INFLUENCE OF UNCERTAINTY ON BUSINESS PLANNING

I. INTRODUCTION

DOWN to this point it has been assumed in this essay that entrepreneurial estimates are subjectively certain: that the entrepreneur thinks he knows—whether he actually does or not—just what will happen if he follows any contemplated business policy.

This simplifying assumption has done a great deal to smooth our path so far. But of course entrepreneurs in fact know that their estimates may be in error and recognize a number of contingencies as possible for any particular policy they may set out to follow. This fact must now be allowed for; uncertainty must be brought in as an essential part of the background of business planning.

It is uncertainty rather than risk (properly so called) which will be of primary interest to us; but a definition of the latter concept is called for, if only to delimit the problem.

Estimates about any future event which is not regarded as certain may involve either uncertainty or risk. The event viewed in isolation is always uncertain. But viewed as a member of a group of events so related that their joint outcome is more certain than the individual events in the group, it is a risk. Both to a fire insurance company and to its owner the future of a building (whether it will burn up or not) is uncertain. But to the company which insures it, assuming that it also insures many comparable buildings, the burning of the building is a risk.

Within a firm, risk situations in the narrow sense exist only where there is room for "self-insurance"—i.e., where the firm carries on a number of separate and comparable operations whose outcomes are independent (say, a large number of shipments by truck subject to hazards of wreck). But firms often succeed in balancing against each other contingencies which are so different qualitatively as not to constitute a "group" in the normal sense. The firm which insures its building against fire knows that a certain favorable contingency—collection of money from the insurance company—will occur if and only if a certain unfavorable contingency—burning of the building—happens to develop. From the standpoint of profit, this knowledge will reduce or perhaps even eliminate uncertainties arising from the fire hazard. But of course it will not eliminate uncertainties as to how operations are to be carried on. Insurance has this effect for the firm whether or not the event insured is in principle "insurable."[1]

In forming a picture of entrepreneurial estimation subject to uncertainty, we may begin by thinking of estimates of the receipts corresponding to a given sales schedule. A unique receipts schedule will exist (even ignoring sales promotion) only if the reactions of future markets are supposed known with certainty. For every sales schedule which may be contemplated (such as that represented in Fig. 2, a) each possible course of markets may be represented by a contingent receipts schedule. More generally, there will be a zone (Fig. 2, c) within which receipts may vary. This is to be thought of, however, as the locus of an indefinitely large number of threads (receipts schedules) such as those of Figure 2, b, each assigned some particular degree of probability.[2]

These alternative schedules, in a representative pattern, will be relatively similar for dates in the near future, but grow gradually more and more unlike. That is, the zone of possible receipts will widen through time. Among the possible schedules, some one (P in Fig. 2, c) will of course rank as most probable—that is, more likely to happen than any other schedule in particular—though if the number of contingencies is large it may itself be thought very improbable. This schedule, however, may be very unrepresentative of the set of alternative contingencies corresponding to the contemplated sales schedule. Much more significant is the expectation schedule (E in Fig. 2, c), which may be constructed by estimating receipts for each date under each contingency, weighting by the estimated probability of the contingency, and summing up the results for each date. By construction, this

[1] On the issue of uncertainty versus risk see F. H. Knight, *Risk, Uncertainty and Profit* (Boston, 1921), pp. 46, 206–16; also J. Marschak, "Money and the Theory of Assets," *Economica*, V, No. 19 (new ser.; 1938), 261 ff.

[2] As the curves of Fig. 2, b indicate, each of these "threads" may coincide through parts of its length with one or several others. That is, the entrepreneur may believe any given course of selling-price and receipts during some particular interval to be compatible with any of several courses during other intervals of future time.

schedule must have a discounted value at t_0 identical with the weighted sum of the discounted values of the contingent schedules. It may be expected to resemble the most probable sched-

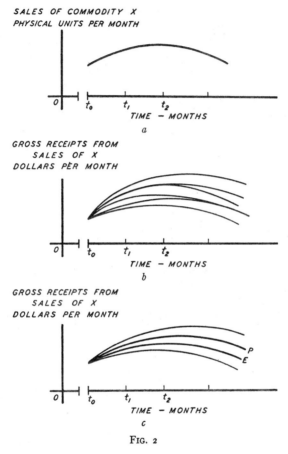

FIG. 2

ule, and it is plausible (though not necessary) to assume it will lie below the latter.

In the above account, as throughout this essay, the entrepreneur's estimates of probability for the different contingencies are assumed to be cardinal numbers (with a total of unity for all possible contingencies, according to the traditional pattern), rather than mere ordinal rankings. That is, the entrepreneur is supposed to think Contingency A not merely more likely than Contingency B but more likely in a definite proportion.

By analogy with the "indifference-curve" theory of the consuming house-hold, it might appear that it would suffice to assume only ordinal probabilities. The writer is not altogether convinced that this is not so. But it is plain that considerations of how much more likely must enter somehow into decisions whether or not a given rate of insurance premiums is "fair" enough to justify taking out insurance (to give a simple illustration); and to express this fact without reference to cardinal probabilities evidently calls for very subtle reasoning if it is possible at all. Even the best attempt at this sort of reasoning with which the writer is acquainted (Dr. Jacob Marschak's article cited above) seems to leave motivation incomplete.

To the reader who would prefer an ordinal system, two consolations may be offered: (1) Since cardinal comparisons are a special case of ordinal comparisons, the results here reached must be some sort of first approximation to the results ordinal analysis would yield; and experience with consumption theory suggests that the corrections (if possible) would not revolutionize the results. (2) As Dr. Tintner has suggested to the writer, allowance for uncertainty may make it necessary to revert to cardinal assumptions in consumption theory. Try the exercise, for example, of deducing from an indifference map relating beefsteak and leisure how many hours of work an individual will do at a certain wage-rate if the price of beefsteak for his dinner is uncertain.

This pattern of contingent estimation may be carried back through the firm's planning. For a given input plan a field of output contingencies can be laid out, each with its field of receipts contingencies. For each input plan, likewise, a field of outlay contingencies can be laid out.

A simple solution of the planning problem may now appear possible by simply substituting expectation schedules for the contingency fields and applying the rules of chapter iii. The procedure, starting with input, would be to find the expectation schedule of output and then locate the expectation schedule of receipts which would correspond to that production schedule. Subtracting from this the expectation schedule of outlays corresponding to the input plan would yield an expectation schedule of net receipts for that input plan which could be reduced to a discounted value. Comparison of these discounted values, finally, would appear to be a guide to choice among the alternative input plans.

This procedure, if satisfactory, would enable us to evade the entire issue of uncertainty. But it is not satisfactory. It implies two unacceptable assumptions about the businessman's attitude, namely:

1. He concerns himself with no aspects of the probability distributions he is dealing with except their mean or expectation values. Even as concerns contingencies regarding net receipts, this is unplausible: the entrepreneur may feel either "risk aversion" or a liking for danger.[3] Further, it can be shown[4] that the expectation value of net receipts may depend on the dispersion of prices or gross receipts rather than merely on their expectation value.

2. He must work out a business plan in full at t_0 and fix it for the life of the firm. This is evidently not merely unnecessary but even foolish business policy. Fuller information about the future will come in as it draws toward the present; and many decisions can be postponed until the information is available. A rule which tells how to lay plans if plans must be irrevocable applies, therefore, only to a wholly fictitious case.

Either of these two considerations would be enough to prevent us from disposing of the uncertainty problem in the cavalier way just sketched. But the writer proposes to waive the first for the moment, reserving it for discussion in the last section of this chapter, and to concentrate for the present on the effects of the second.

The central phenomena of uncertainty, in the writer's view, would arise even in a world where everyone was neutral toward danger or even welcomed it, so long as willingness to sacrifice prospective income in order to "live dangerously" did not become absolute. These central phenomena relate to the preservation of flexibility in planning, with a view to making the most of later opportunities to improve estimates. Allowance for "risk aversion" is best made after this stage of analysis is completed.

[3] J. R. Hicks (*Value and Capital* [Oxford, 1939], pp. 125–26) proposes that "we must not take the most probable [sic] price as the representative expected price, but the most probable price ± an allowance for the uncertainty of the expectation, that is to say, an allowance for risk"; but this is plainly inadequate.

[4] Cf. the writer's article, "Risk, Uncertainty, and the Unprofitability of Compounding Probabilities," in the forthcoming volume of essays in memory of Professor Henry Schultz, which contains a mathematical special-case analysis showing that higher moments of price distributions are likely to affect the expectation of profit distributions.

II. UNCERTAINTY OF INDEPENDENT EVENTS

As a first stage in the argument, it is proposed to analyze a special case simplified to the absolute limit beyond which scope for flexibility would vanish. It is assumed: (a) that the firm sells but a single product; (b) that there is no uncertainty of technology, buying-prices, or interest-rates; (c) that the amount of goods available for sale on a future date t_k is entirely unaffected by operations looking toward sales of other dates; (d) that the selling-market at t_k is unaffected by sales of other dates, or by the firm's purchases; and (e) that the firm is not subject to capital-rationing. These assumptions, of course, are merely for illustration.

To give a basis of comparison, we may first assume that the entrepreneur must decide at t_0 just how much to produce for sale at the later date t_k. This implies either that no further information is expected or that technology commits the entrepreneur to immediate decision. In either event, the case is covered by the pseudo-solution described above.

The situation may readily be expressed by a two-dimensional diagram (Fig. 3). For each scale of output (=sales) there will by our assumptions be an unambiguously defined optimum input plan—that which offers minimum discounted value of outlays. This permits us to reckon total costs for each level of output (curve TC of Fig. 3). Marketing expectations may be shown by curves r_1, r_2, and r_3, showing receipts under all the various contingencies imagined possible. The expectation curve R is the weighted sum of the contingent curves. Under these conditions the optimum output is that for which R lies furthest above TC: that is, the entrepreneur should behave as though the expectation shown by curve R were single valued.

If the entrepreneur expects further information, however, and if he is free to alter his provisional plan when the information comes in, there is a different answer. Suppose, e.g., that his technology, schedules of buying-prices, and initial selling-market estimates are the same as before, but that he is certain at t_0 that by date t_f further information will make it sure which of the contingent selling-market situations will exist at t_k. His problem is to select not a final but a provisional output.

The new cost situation may be represented by a pair of curves (Fig. 4). Besides the original curve TC, which shows the cost of

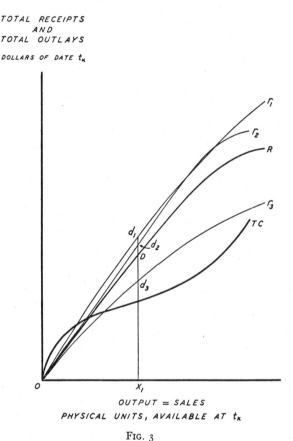

TOTAL   RECEIPTS
AND
TOTAL   OUTLAYS

DOLLARS OF DATE t_k

OUTPUT = SALES
PHYSICAL UNITS , AVAILABLE AT t_k

FIG. 3

each possible output if operations from t_0 to t_f are ideally adapted to that output, we may draw a revised cost curve $C'C'$ showing the cost of each output if operations down to date t_f are adapted to an output x_m and operations from t_f to t_k modified to fit the output in question. By construction, the two curves must coincide for $x = x_m$, and $C'C'$ must lie higher than TC for other outputs. The vertical distance between the curves will represent the cost of shifting from output x_m to the final output. This will be greater as the size of the shift is greater and as date t_f is nearer date t_k.

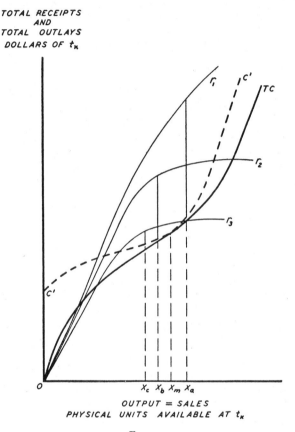

TOTAL RECEIPTS
AND
TOTAL OUTLAYS
DOLLARS OF t_k

OUTPUT = SALES
PHYSICAL UNITS AVAILABLE AT t_k

FIG. 4

When it becomes certain, at t_f, which of the contingent revenue curves will become actual, output will be selected so as to find the greatest excess of revenue above costs measured on $C'C'$—giving output of either x_a or x_b or x_c in the case represented by Figure 4. Owing to the cost of shifting—which will raise marginal costs for outputs above x_m and lower them for outputs below x_m—the optimum output in each contingency will lie between x_m and the output which would have been planned if the corresponding revenue curve had been certain from the outset.

The $C'C'$ curve of Figure 4 will be different according to the value of x_m selected. As x_m increases, the left-hand branch of $C'C'$ will rise and the right-hand branch will fall. In choosing the provisional output x_m, therefore, the entrepreneur is choosing among alternative cost curves, some of which are more favorable for smaller and some for larger outputs. He should select that provisional output whose $C'C'$ curve offers the largest expectation of net receipts on the original set of contingent selling-market estimates, allowing for shifting and for its costs. This is not in general the same as the output which would be chosen in the light of the same set of anticipations if shifting from the provisional output were barred.[5]

Once we recognize that the entrepreneur has a choice among cost curves, it becomes plain that he may reach a cost curve with better prospects of net receipts by following a plan of operations from t_0 to t_f which would not be precisely the optimum for any particular final output determined in advance. Presumably there will always be an output x_m to which the provisional plan is better adapted than to any other. But ordinarily it will be worth while to adopt a plan which makes $C'C'$ higher than TC at output $x = x_m$ in order to reduce the cost of shifting in the more likely event that some final output other than x_m will be selected.

This policy of flexibility will of course yield worse results than immediate decision based upon following a "hunch" as to the final market situation if the "hunch" happens to be correct. But if it is not correct—a much more likely supposition—flexibility will yield much better results. Unless costs of shifting are prohibitive or the market contingencies very nearly identical, flexibility will raise the expectation of net receipts.

Having once established for this simple case the principle that under uncertainty the prospects of net receipts can be improved by planning for flexibility, it is not hard to extend the results and

[5] For an example of this difference see the writer's article in the volume of essays in memory of Henry Schultz, referred to above.

eliminate the first two of the special assumptions made above.[6] The existence of several types of output, uncertainty of technology, uncertainty of buying-prices and of interest rates, will plainly increase rather than decrease the inducements to lay plans so as to leave room for changes; and no special proof of the point need be offered.

Another special assumption of the last few paragraphs—that the entrepreneur's estimates at t_0 combine uncertain guesses as to final prices with complete assurance that these prices will be definitely known at t_f—is almost as easy to dispose of. It is obvious that the argument would be identical in substance, though needing an extra stage, if the information due at t_f would only reduce the number of contingencies still to be treated as possibilities, certainly not arriving until a date t_g, between t_f and t_k. For each distribution of t_f estimates considered possible at t_0, there would be an optimum provisional plan for operations between t_f and t_g; and the problem at the outset would be to adopt a plan for operations between t_0 and t_f which would give the best choice of cost curves when t_f came around. The same argument could be applied if the *convergence* of expectations involved a large number of successive stages. Since it is certainly plausible to assume convergence—i.e., to suppose that accumulating information makes the markets of t_k predictable within a smaller and smaller range as t_k approaches —the desirability of flexibility does not depend on the simplification of assuming certainty to arrive at t_f.

It is more difficult, however, to generalize for the effect of interrelations between dates in technology and marketing and even more for the effect of capital-rationing. These two tasks will be undertaken in the two succeeding sections of this chapter.

III. INTERRELATIONS BETWEEN DATES IN THE UNCERTAINTY PROBLEM

Technology creates several kinds of linkage between goods available for sale at different dates: (*a*) output once produced may commonly be stored; hence sales of several dates may be linked with output of one date; (*b*) half-finished goods may be

---

[6] Cf. the list on p. 56 above.

stored, or intermediate products may be durable in use; hence salable output of several dates may be linked with one date's output of intermediate products; and (c) goods purchased may be stored, or may be durable in use; hence service input of several dates may be linked with one date's purchases. The present section of this chapter will be devoted to working out the consequences of these linkages, allowing also for market interrelations of purchases and sales of different dates.

We may begin, as usual, with the selling-market. An entrepreneur whose selling-market is uncertain (we may suppose his buying-markets and capital markets neither uncertain nor rationed) must expect to find his market estimates for given future dates changing as those dates approach. If they do change, his provisional plans for sales must be altered; and advance preparation for such alteration is called for.

Suppose, e.g., that his revision of selling-market estimates is pessimistic. If his provisional sales schedule is maintained, discounted marginal revenue of output for a series of dates will fall short of marginal cost of output. This plainly calls for adopting a lower sales schedule than had been expected (to raise marginal revenue) and a lower production schedule than had been expected (to lower marginal cost).

Particularly if there is danger of "spoiling the market" by sudden price cuts, rapid curtailment of sales is likely to be advisable. But if a new provisional sales schedule is established lying some distance below the old, it is likely to be cheapest in terms of processing costs to cut output less than sales for dates near the time when estimates are revised, more than sales for dates more remote.[7] To do so, however, calls for existence of storage facilities. Where the product will stand storage, holding a reserve of storage space is a first step toward flexibility.

In case the revision in estimates is optimistic, however, mere empty storage space will not be sufficient. To adjust the sales schedule more rapidly than production, the firm must have a stock of salable goods on hand. Preparedness to take advantage of such favorable market developments thus requires planning to

[7] See the discussion of flexibility under certainty above, pp. 25–27, 50.

carry some inventory constantly, in excess of seasonal require-ments, in the event that markets develop no better than ex-pected.

A similar device for maintaining flexibility of the sales sched-ule—applicable particularly where final product is hard to store—is maintenance of a normal inventory of materials or half-finished goods, together with a margin of unused plant capacity for work-ing them up on short notice at reasonable cost. This device, how-ever, requires also flexibility in the productive operations lying between the goods stocked and the salable product, which is an inconvenience unless those operations are only part of the firm's activities.

As among provisional production plans for turning out a given list of types of salable output, uncertainty of the selling-market puts a premium on plans which lend themselves to revision with-out loss. More concretely, selling-market uncertainty—as com-pared with certain expectations having the same expectation values—will make it desirable to keep down holdings of durable equipment, to avoid long-term buying-contracts, to choose proc-esses under which the intermediate products are of unspecialized form and capable of storage, and to choose processes under which the bulk of the service input for output of given date is post-poned until that date comes near.

In the event that markets follow the course marked out by ex-pectation schedules, such a plan will yield lower net receipts than would a plan based on the assumption that expectations were certain to be fulfilled. But in exchange the firm will have higher net receipts in the more likely event that it has to adapt itself to markets better or worse than expectations. How far it is worth sacrificing the former advantage to the latter will obviously de-pend both upon the technical opportunities for flexibility and upon the degree of dispersion of market anticipations about the ex-pectation.

If all the possible market contingencies are very much alike, and if a flexible program offers very high costs in case expecta-tions are confirmed, flexibility will not be carried far. If the range of reasonably probable market contingencies is large, and if flexibility offers only small disadvantages in case expectations are confirmed, flexibility will be pressed to the limit.[8]

Similar considerations affect the choice of products. Higher expectation value of income in the event that expectations for markets are fulfilled will make a product relatively attractive; uncertainty of markets combined with low flexibility in production will offer a deterrent. These considerations will have to be balanced against each other (unless they happen both to run in favor of the same product).

Choice of products will also be affected by correlations in selling-market estimates. If there is negative correlation—if there is reason to believe that conditions which make a bad market for one will make a good market for another—they will make a favorable pair of products for the firm; and there will be a premium on flexibility devices making it possible to switch production from one to the other. The same argument applies in less degree if markets are believed independent. If there is positive correlation, no protection can be secured by having multiple products, and the premium will be on flexibility of total operation as if there were only one product.

Uncertainty of buying-markets is so nearly symmetrical with selling-market uncertainty that it need not detain us long. The argument which shows the wastefulness of sudden alterations in production schedules applies also—though with less intensity— to sudden alterations of input.[9] In case of an unexpected stiffening of a buying-market, possession of an inventory of the input in question will permit purchases to be cut off at once, while allowing a gradual adjustment of input which will give time to introduce substitutes.

To be able to take prompt advantage of unexpected favorable buying-price shifts, the firm must be in a position to expand co-operating input. In so far as this co-operating input will spring from goods owned by the firm, a margin of such goods above ex-

---

. [8] An extreme dispersion of market contingencies, however—particularly if it is bimodal, two radically different contingencies being more likely than anything in between—may simply be paralyzing.

[9] See above, pp. 30, 61.

pected requirements will be useful, permitting activity in departments using the goods to rise in advance of their production schedules or purchase schedules. In the choice among processes and among products, moreover, buying-price uncertainty favors plans under which intersubstitution of different purchased input items is easy; for such plans will be readily adaptable to unforeseen relative buying-price changes.

Where buying-markets and selling-markets are both uncertain, it is likely that the uncertainties will be correlated through competition.[10] Often—though of course not always—the firms which compete most closely with a given firm on its selling-markets are also its closest competitors on the markets where it buys; and in such cases productive methods also are likely to be similar. Thus in the lumber business the same firms are competitors for timberland, for qualified labor, and for selling-markets, and most use similar methods. In such circumstances our entrepreneur may fairly expect that contingencies which mean good selling-markets for him will mean the same for his competitors. Accordingly, the same contingencies will stiffen his buying-markets. If selling-prices are unexpectedly high, buying-prices will be so too. On the other hand, contingencies where buying-prices are at the top and selling-prices simultaneously at the bottom of the possible range are wildly improbable.

Like correlation within the pattern of uncertain selling-price anticipations, correlation of this type is a stabilizing influence reducing the need for productive flexibility. It is less important for a meat packer (say) to be able to vary the amount of beef processed without great changes in marginal costs than it would be if the prices of beef and of live cattle were likely to fluctuate in opposite directions.

Although the need of flexibility is reduced, however, it is not eliminated. Buying-prices representing specialized input will be more closely correlated with the firm's selling-prices than buying-

[10] Competition need not be "perfect" or "pure" to introduce such a correlation. Note that this intrusion of interfirm relations takes the form of a hypothesis about the entrepreneur's estimates and does not involve events, so that it does not take us beyond the scope outlined for this essay.

prices representing input widely used by firms with noncompeting output. Consequently there remains a problem of capturing the benefits of favorable surprises on selling-markets by expanding unspecialized input, which will not rise in price with output; while if selling-markets turn out badly the same considerations point toward curtailing unspecialized more than specialized input. To create such substitution possibilities requires planning for flexibility.

The fact that uncertainty—specifically, a high dispersion of anticipations around the expectation—favors processes under which durable equipment, etc., will be held to a minimum lends color to the widely held view that an increase of uncertainty will act upon the firm like an increase in interest rates. But this parallel is readily overstrained.

It is not correct to infer, e.g., that a decrease in the dispersion of market anticipations (with constant expectation value and constant interest) will cause the firm to demand more outside financing, as would a fall of interest with market anticipations unchanged. For while a reduced degree of uncertainty might make it worth investing more capital in fixed form, it would also release part of the capital previously tied up in cash balances[11] and in inventories. Even with fixed capital, furthermore, higher specialization might reduce costs: for instance, an industrial building whose uses are definitely foreknown can prudently be constructed with lighter floors than one which may have to be transferred to other uses. This release of capital may quite possibly outweigh the absorption through greater use of durable specialized equipment.

Another analogy frequently drawn—that future sums are "discounted" not merely to allow for futurity but to allow for uncertainty—has its uses but is too easily stretched to unwarranted lengths. True, if the firm's explicit estimates of future net receipts under a contemplated plan run in terms merely of the most probable course of future receipts,[12] a biased error is introduced which can be crudely corrected by raising the rate of discount. The

[11] See below, pp. 69–71.

[12] An interpretation suggested to the writer by Professor T. O. Yntema.

reason is that the schedule of most probable net receipts will commonly lie more and more above the expectation schedule as the date for which estimates are made becomes more remote. But in a more refined analysis, where all contingencies are allowed for, the appropriate rate of discounting will not be affected by the degree of uncertainty of buying- and selling-prices.

Uncertainty, of course, does not apply merely to markets: technology may also be uncertain. Here we have two major problems to deal with: (a) There may be uncertainty of input-output relations *within* the range of productive methods now in use. (b) There may be uncertainty as to the methods which will be available in future. It is also uncertain, of course, whether buildings will burn, employees be hurt, trucks be damaged, money be stolen, etc.; but, as will appear in the next section of this chapter, such uncertainties fall rather paradoxically under the heading of capital-market uncertainty rather than technological uncertainty.

To begin with uncertainty of the output obtainable under present methods from given input, this has several subtypes. It may depend on uncertain natural events (weather in farming; movements of shoals in fishing). It may hinge on unknown properties of the firm's outfit (thickness of veins in mining; hidden defects leading to breakdown of manufacturing or transport equipment). Or it may arise simply from laying out activities a bit beyond the range in which the firm's engineering experience has been tested by recent experience.

Assuming a perfect capital market and no risk aversion, uncertain technological anticipations of this general type may be represented by their expectation values unless there are chances of mitigating them by being in a position to shift methods in case of unexpected developments. How far some chances exist the engineer can judge better than the economist; but certainly they do exist in some sectors. In horticulture, for instance, it is possible— at a cost—to hedge against uncertain rainfall by preparing for irrigation; and in extending the geographical range of orange-growing, the smudge pot is a partial substitute for certainty of temperature. In manufacturing, variants of untried methods which use existing equipment have obvious advantages over variants calling for special installations, since they make it easier to revert to the old system in case of failure.

Uncertainty of future methods is a subject little discussed among economic theorists—presumably because it so obviously involves going outside the traditional "static" framework. But it is plain that entrepreneurs must know that methods will change, and even more plain that they cannot believe they know just how they will change.[13] Economists, furthermore, are in a position to make some inferences as to the effect of this uncertainty.

The key to the puzzle is that expectation of technical change involves a forecast of deterioration in selling-markets or buying-markets or both. For as competitors either devise new methods or develop parallels to methods devised by our firm, they will be able to make more favorable offers to our firm's customers and suppliers.

To protect itself in this situation, the firm needs a research department, or a system of espionage to learn the methods of others, or both. It needs to be able to expand and take advantage of its opportunities if it pulls ahead in the competitive race of discovery. If it drops behind, the contracting spread between buying- and selling-prices will squeeze it out of existence—unless it can maintain itself by using largely resources which are not useful in the new process and therefore drop in price, like the services of glassblowers some decades ago; and against this contingency it is good policy to keep assets in relatively unspecialized form, to reduce losses in liquidation.

IV. UNCERTAINTY COMBINED WITH CAPITAL-RATIONING

Down to this point the discussion of this chapter has assumed the capital market to be both perfect and certain. But there is no reason why it need be either; and, if it is not, important analytical consequences follow. In particular, dropping these assumptions enables us to motivate the businessman's craving for "liquidity" and his willingness to buy insurance at rates including heavy charges for administration and for fraudulent losses.

---

[13] Such a notion, in fact, would involve a contradiction in terms; for a future method perfectly foreknown would be a present method.

To begin with imperfection—rather than uncertainty—of the capital market, for a firm subject to capital-rationing there is a type of interrelation between operations of different dates which we have not yet considered. Success or failure of operations at early dates affects the firm's ability to finance later operations. A gain in the near future will permit a larger and presumably more profitable scale of operations later on; a loss in the near future will require planning smaller operations for the remote future. Prospects of net receipts for the remaining life of the firm, therefore, will be affected by immediate losses and gains.

These relations, furthermore, are assymetrical. The reason is that immediate losses outrunning some fraction of the firm's net worth will throw it into bankruptcy. An uninsured fire loss (e.g.) of half the net worth will dangerously reduce the margin of safety of the firm's creditors. If they take alarm, a forced sale will ensue; and the liquidation value of the firm's assets sold piecemeal (or sold as a whole without due notice) will be far below their going-concern value. Losses of this character, then, may magnify themselves by causing the net worth to evaporate, under capital-rationing, whereas with a theoretical perfect capital market (creditors feeling certainty) loan funds would be obtainable so long as the firm's going-concern value exceeded its debts, and the secondary loss could not happen. This characteristic of losses under capital-rationing has no counterpart in the event of immediate gains, unless the firm is already in a position where only such gains can avert bankruptcy.

This assymetry makes it rational to insure at rates which exceed "actuarial values"—as all insurance rates must do, in view of administration costs, unless the insurance company's preventive measures make insured firms much safer "risks" than uninsured firms. If the entrepreneur estimates the probability of our illustrative fire loss at 0.01, and if the secondary losses will equal the fire loss, he can "rationally" pay up to 2 per cent insurance premium;[14] for the existence of insurance will prevent creditors from

---

[14] The existence of indirect losses in case of uninsured fire losses, etc., is clearly recognized by G. Myrdal (see *Prisbildningsproblemet och Föränderligheten* [Uppsala,

taking fright. Paying more than actuarial rates, then, may be evidence of capital-rationing rather than of "risk aversion."

Similar considerations make it worth while for a firm subject to capital-rationing to maintain "liquidity"—i.e., to have cash balances and unused borrowing-power in excess of what will be used if events follow the expectation values of estimates. In our example of the fire loss, if the firm's debt were far below conventional ratios, it would have been able to borrow and keep its going-concern value alive, avoiding secondary losses. Liquidity is thus a partial substitute for insurance; and for many types of losses, against which insurance is not purchasable, it is the only protection.

Liquidity, moreover, can adapt the firm for favorable contingencies, as insurance cannot. Economies in buying depend largely on having a flexible purchase plan, therefore on having prompt access to funds. This side of the matter is probably less important than ability to weather unfavorable contingencies—since the favorable turn of markets itself enhances the firm's borrowing-power —but it has a good deal of weight where goods bought will stand storage.

Both liquidity and the practice of carrying insurance, furthermore, improve the firm's credit rating and thus increase its rationing-allowance of outside funds and sometimes reduce rationing-rates of interest. Increasing the amount of "liquid" assets held, accordingly, need not much decrease the amount of other types of assets; and paying insurance premiums or paying interest on funds held idle need not much impair the firm's net receipts in fair weather, while offering substantial improvement if events do not follow expectations.

Besides necessitating capital-rationing, the forces which prevent perfection of the capital market also limit the firm's opportunities for outside investment. By charter limitations or otherwise most firms are subjected to investment taboos. If the firm

1927], pp. 148–49). But he speaks of these losses as due to "tidsmoment i prisbildningströgheten"—i.e., "lags in price adjustment"—rather than to capital-rationing.

has excess of resources over what its business plan requires—which implies bearish forecasts for its normal markets—there are but few forms of property it is allowed to buy. Under American conditions government securities (perhaps only of short maturities) sometimes exhaust the list; and at most it will take in land and commodities of types similar to those used in normal operations, possibly shares of corporations in related branches of business.

This enhances the likelihood that a bearish attitude on the part of management will cause the firm to hold idle cash. It is not necessary that this bearishness should apply to all assets, as it would have to if the firm's investment powers were unlimited. It is enough if it covers the full list of eligible assets—or even if the entrepreneur is doubtful that the eligible assets will rise in price.

All these inducements to hold cash (or carry insurance) are accentuated for concerns in which there is a conflict of "insider" and "outsider" interests, with a resulting tendency to sacrifice the latter to the former. The "outsider," inevitably, is in a poor position to judge the intensity of the hazards against which these devices protect the firm. If too much is paid for protection, then—within conventional limits—the "outsiders" are unlikely to resent it. On the other hand, occurrence of an uninsured loss that could have been covered—even though premiums quoted were exorbitant—will give them a grievance against the management. In many concerns the "insiders" are so insecure that such an event may endanger their position. As the proportion of outside capital increases, this hazard to the "insiders" grows stronger, and at the same time the proportion of the cost of protection which can be assessed upon the "outsiders" increases; so that there is a double inducement to be more "conservative" than the joint interests of all security-holders would require.

Where bearish prospects for the firm's operations tend to enlarge cash holdings, a similar temptation exists for the "insiders" to overdo it. Since the security-holders, as individuals, have a wider range of permitted types of investments than the firm, there is a presumption that in their interest the redundant cash of the firm should be distributed. This is sometimes prevented by charter provisions against "unearned" dividends. But even where there are no such barriers, the "insiders"—who gain in many ways from ruling a large rather than a small firm—have a motive to prevent disbursements in order to increase the scale of operations later.[15]

In the last few paragraphs we have ignored uncertainty of the capital market—except as under capital-rationing operating uncertainty leads to uncertainty of the future scale of operations, and this amounts to capital-market uncertainty.

In recent monetary discussions[16] capital-market uncertainty—i.e., uncertainty of interest rates—has been held forth as a motive for liquidity. A firm engaged in construction of a plant, e.g., may prefer to float bonds at once and hold idle cash for a while rather than borrow on short term as work progresses and fund the debt at completion, if its interest forecasts are uncertain. But, in addition to interest uncertainty, the explanation of such behavior requires either an assumption of risk aversion (which will be considered in the next section) or else an assumption of capital-rationing creating dangers of secondary losses. Otherwise, it is hard to see why chances of lower interest rates should not balance risks of higher rates, if the rate now offered corresponds to the expectation value of estimates.

Uncertainty in a capital market subject to rationing is most likely, of course, to be uncertainty about rationing-allowances; and uncertainty of this character adds greatly to the inducements to be liquid. A reduction of the firm's own allowance might strip it of working capital: to be sure of having a margin of liquidity thus calls for less use of existing borrowing-power, particularly on short term, or on long term with bunched maturities. Changes in capital-rationing applied by others to the firm's customers, more-

---

[15] There seems to be general acceptance for the hypothesis that, if stockholders once lay their hands on the money, management can never persuade them to reinvest it; this was the foundation for much of the clamor against the ill-starred "undistributed profits tax."

[16] Cf. J. M. Keynes, *General Theory of Employment, Interest and Money* (New York, 1936), pp. 168–70, 201–2; G. L. S. Shackle, *Expectations, Investment and Income* (London, 1938), pp. 49–53. Both these authors, however, look at uncertainty of interest rates primarily from the standpoint of the rentier rather than of the entrepreneur.

over, may affect their demand for credit. Against both these hazards liquidity protects the firm by increasing its adaptability; and against the first liquidity also erects the bulwark of a reputation for conservatism.

V. "AVERSION TO RISK"

Uncertainty reactions—in particular, the taking-out of insurance, the maintenance of liquidity, and the bias in favor of unspecialized equipment—are commonly thought of as devices by which the standard deviation of net receipts prospects is reduced at the expense of reducing their expectation value.[17] To explain the willingness of businessmen to make this supposed sacrifice of income expectations, "risk aversion" is attributed to them, in the face of much evidence that in some quarters danger is courted.

This view of the uncertainty reactions, as we have seen, is inadequate. They *may* be, and commonly are, devices for raising the expectation value of net receipts for the life of the firm by reducing their standard deviation for the near future. Risk aversion, then, is not necessary for their explanation.

If it does exist, however, risk aversion will plainly affect the policy of the firm. And there are two important reasons for believing that entrepreneurs cannot ordinarily be neutral toward risk.

The first of these reasons is the presumption that the owners of the firm, in their personal capacity, will have risk aversion because of the much-maligned principle of diminishing utility—which despite their protestations most theorists probably continue to believe in. There is a strong presumption that a household which is to have a given average income over (say) the next ten years will be better off if its flow is approximately even than if it fluctuates very widely.[18] As between a larger average with wide fluctuations and a slightly smaller average with narrow fluctuations, the latter is likely to yield greater "total satisfac-

---

[17] For examples of this attitude cf. the passages cited in n. 16 above.

[18] This need not imply that *complete* stability is the optimum. Aside from possible changes in family composition, tastes, etc., it is possible that the very process of adaptation to changing income may give a certain zest to life. Planning activity, in moderation, is very agreeable. But this consideration will not apply below a certain minimum level of income (depending on social conventions), or for changes either of great frequency or of great amplitude.

tion." This presumption is strengthened if the fluctuations are not altogether predictable; for unexpected changes of income in either direction cause some past expenditures to go to waste.

Individuals who draw their incomes largely from a single firm, consequently, will normally want the income of the firm to be stable and certain; and of course in general measures for increased certainty will also give increased stability. This pressure will be significant, however, only for private firms and closely held corporations. Corporations in which individual investors are not deeply committed are not touched by it.

The second reason for doubting risk neutrality is the obvious emotional halo surrounding danger and security. Exposure to danger is the source of the highly valued utility called a "thrill"— the chief product of large sectors of the amusement industry and of sport.[19] Dangerous activity is more interesting and—if the participants have a chance to show their courage—more dignified than secure activity.

On the other hand, "security" is ardently longed for and has erected its economic monuments in life insurance and the Social Security Act. Both these apparently conflicting desires seem to be well-nigh universal, though their relative strength seems to differ from person to person. Some economic institutions (and some classes of firms) appeal to one, some to the other. There is a fair presumption that holders of American Telephone and Telegraph shares and of British investment trusts are looking for security and want conservative administration; while holders of American investment trusts and mining shares want "a run for their money." If a firm adopts either a policy of conservatism or a policy of dashing boldness, natural selection will tend to attach to it a body of stockholders who will want that policy continued.

If a firm's management does wish to sacrifice income to security, the devices open to it are precisely those discussed in the earlier sections of this chapter. Liberal use of insurance, high liquidity inventories of nonperishable goods, choice of products and mate-

---

[19] Note, however, the curiously ambiguous quality of the "thrill": at least for many individuals, an underlying sense that the danger is not real makes it more enjoyable. It is agreeable to be secure enough to feel some detachment and to savor the danger. Hence, presumably, the peculiar charms of vicarious danger in sport, motion pictures, the drama, and war news.

rials with stable markets, unspecialized equipment, etc., are called for; they should simply be carried somewhat further than if the maximum expectation of income is sought.

On the other hand, a firm whose management prefers danger should stop short of the maximum-income level of precaution. In particular, it should adopt new products and risky processes, appealing for support to investors who want adventure and take direct satisfaction in association with a concern having high research and engineering standards.

Some years ago the writer was interviewed by an amateur economist with a project for organizing hundreds of small corporations to develop and exploit new inventions, the shares to be sold at a few cents each to the sort of people who now buy lottery tickets, etc. His hypothesis was that such ventures could give people more enjoyment than lotteries (particularly if they put out attractive prospectuses!), could offer as good a chance of big prizes as a lottery, and could make productive use of funds which now are poured down a rathole. Many less meritorious schemes have come from supposedly authoritative sources!

Where a desire to avoid or to court danger is at work simultaneously with the factors above described—expectation of further information and capital-market imperfection—its effects will be qualitatively indistinguishable from theirs. It can be argued, of course, that if certain branches of industry are unattractive on account of "risk," returns to capital and management will tend to be unusually high in those branches (whether the attractiveness consists in too much danger or too little). But, unfortunately, the same effect might result either from a bias in accounting systems, from a greater stringency of capital-rationing, or from a tendency toward overpessimism (by some objective standard) among people considering that industry. A tendency to make overconservative plans from given estimates has an obvious psychological affinity with a tendency to make pessimistic estimates; but the two are not the same thing.

Neither the nature of the precautions taken, therefore, nor accounting records of the results can tell us in what combinations risk aversion and other uncertainty factors are at work. In interpretation of events we must rely on other types of evidence to tell us which way the experience points. But it is a safe presumption that both classes of factors are quantitatively important.

CHAPTER V

THE ORIGIN AND REVISION OF ANTICIPATIONS

I. SOURCES OF ESTIMATES

T HE argument of this essay so far has taken the entrepreneur's estimates—including elements of uncertainty—as data. Adaptation of plans to revised anticipations has been considered; but we have not seriously considered how anticipations come to be revised.

But the objective of the essay is to work out a theory of the firm which will lend itself to the study of business fluctuations and money; and this commits us to an attempt at explaining anticipations, even though complete success may not be expected. As J. R. Hicks has pointed out,[1] the academic economist's very real handicaps in deriving anticipations from the observables on which they must in principle be based cannot excuse him from making the attempt; though they do put him under obligation to collaborate with others better versed in "business psychology."

The brief sketch presented in this chapter limits itself almost entirely to the collection and systematization of rather obvious considerations which must lie very close to the surface of most current economic thinking. While it is hoped that the result will offer some guidance for further analysis, the reader is put on notice that the materials used are very fragmentary and the conclusions drawn very tentative. This is a field in which a well-balanced program of theoretical and institutional research could work wonders.

If we confine ourselves for the moment to technological estimates, the question whence anticipations spring and how and why they come to be revised is fairly manageable.

In general, the knowledge which can be mustered among the firm's own personnel—together with such "outside" sources as

---

[1] Cf. pp. 13–14 of his "Suggestion for Simplifying the Theory of Money," *Economica*, February, 1935, and also the remarks of G. L. S. Shackle, cited above, p. 7.

weather forecasts and advice from engineering consultants—gives a sufficient foundation for these estimates. Occasionally it is necessary to allow for the activities of other firms, as when a farmer takes account of pests engendered on neighboring farms, or a mine manager of the effect of pumping operations in other mines on his drainage problems. But interfirm influences are rarely of the first order of importance.

Marketing estimates, on the other hand, are in their essence estimates of the behavior of individuals or firms outside the entrepreneur's control. The firm cannot sell unless there is a buyer or buy unless there is a seller; and it cannot estimate its markets without forecasting their actions. This fact sets the framework for our inquiry.

If the firm is so fortunate as to know definitely who its customers and suppliers will be, its problem is to forecast the plans of these particular dealers—not, of course, as these plans exist at the date of estimation but as they will exist when the time for the transaction comes. If it is not certain with whom the firm will deal, a larger circle of potential customers and suppliers must be covered—either as individuals or as groups—by the firm's estimates. In either case, allowance must be made not only for the willingness of suppliers to sell and customers to buy but also for the extent to which the firm's competitors will satisfy this willingness.

In case the firm's markets happen to be completely impersonal and highly competitive, it is formally adequate to estimate buying and selling prices. But this situation is far from universal; and even where it exists, the content of the price estimate is at least implicitly an estimate of dealer behavior.

Businessmen often have at their disposal a good deal of direct information about the plans of other firms for the nearer future. Transactions with customers and with suppliers are often covered by more or less definite agreements (ranging from contracts en forcible at law to vague intimations of intention). Even competitors pool information to some extent.[2] But unless there is a contract, this sort of information is at best a description—not guar-

---

[2] This is one of the main functions of trade associations.

anteed accurate—of provisional plans subject to change. The description may be very inaccurate or even deliberately falsified. Ordinarily, moreover, it will not cover transactions far enough into the future to be a guide to long-term commitments. For all these reasons it is prudent to supplement direct information—where it exists—by independent estimates.

Given sufficient information, an interpreneur may be able to deduce the character of another firm's plans. This requires some knowledge of the other firm's technology and plant, access to its sources of market information, and some basis for inferring what its practices of estimation and planning are. Such a plan reconstruction may be accompanied by an estimate as to the correctness of the other firm's market anticipations—taking account of information the other firm may lack and of the temperament of those responsible for its estimates—leading to a forecast as to whether experience will or will not confirm the estimates. If it will not, a forecast of the resulting revised version of anticipations and plans is called for.

When the number of dealers is small, the entrepreneur is likely to have direct knowledge of the personalities and habits of other dealers which will give his forecasts a decided advantage over those of "outsiders." When numbers are larger and personal acquaintance thus less useful, specialists in market analysis are often used. Sometimes they are hired as full-time employees; sometimes their services are bought "by the piece" in the form of special reports, statistical bulletins, "Washington letters," or what not.

Market forecasts may also be attempted by mere projection into the future of recent market history. Only an entrepreneur dealing on very impersonal markets can afford to rely on this technique to the complete neglect of plan reconstruction. On the other hand, no set of estimates can be constructed without some use of this extrapolation technique. In estimating the factors influencing his customers and suppliers—or, if his estimates go deeper, the factors influencing their customers and suppliers—he is bound to come to variables he can forecast in no other way.[3]

[3] It makes a great difference, of course, at what level the estimator falls back on extrapolation. To take an example from business-cycle theory, a shipbuilder in the

In forecasting by extrapolation, unfortunately, there is no golden rule. Instead, we have three basic assumptions, which may be applied in an infinite number of combinations: (a) that the recent level of the variable under study will continue; (b) that the recent rate of change of the variable will continue —an assumption which admits of variants, as we may consider the significant rate of change to be either the rate of growth or the rate of acceleration, or some higher derivative; and (c) that the variable will tend toward some level thought of as "normal." These three assumptions, curiously and wonderfully mixed, lie at the root of most forecasts.

The three rules of extrapolation all run parallel for a short way in the interpretation of unexpected changes in things of immediate concern to the firm. If, for example, it has sold slightly more than expected (at the expected price) in the last week, this points toward more optimistic anticipations for later weeks—assuming always that no special reason has been discovered for the pleasant surprise which cannot act in later weeks. If the recent sales volume is projected at a constant level, the level is higher because of the surprise; if the rate of change of sales is projected, it is rising more rapidly (or falling more slowly) than previously thought; if the sales volume is expected to drift toward a norm, it will start from a higher level.

But while all three rules may agree as to the direction of the revision, they will not agree as to the distance it should extend into the future, or as to intensity. Projection of the level of sales, in our example, points toward parallel revision of sales estimates for all dates by a like number (say) of tons per week. Projection of the rate of change points toward revision in the same direction for all dates but by a much larger amount for later dates. Assuming a drift toward a norm—if the experience has not affected the norm—points toward revision in the same direction for all dates in the near and middle future, but by a smaller amount for later dates, with no revision at all for dates after the normal situation

early stages of business revival would draw much more optimistic conclusions by extrapolating recent increases in ship sales than by extrapolating recent rises in shipments by sea and deducing the future market for ships.

is expected to be restored. Whether experience will affect the norm depends largely on whether the unexpected movement was toward it or away from it. In the former case, confidence in it will be confirmed; in the latter case, it may be thought that the norm was misplaced.[4]

Since we have no simple rule for the way in which the different patterns of extrapolation will be combined, we have no good way of generalizing the effect of a firm's direct experience on its estimates. All we know in general is that disagreeable surprises point toward pessimistic revision of anticipations; agreeable surprises, toward optimistic revision.[5]

An apparent solution for this indeterminancy is offered by J. R. Hicks's concept of the "elasticity of expectations" or "ratio of the proportional rise in expected future price of X to the proportionate rise in its current price." But Professor Hicks himself puts this forward as a basis of classification which is satisfactory only excluding "the possibility that a change in the current price of X may affect to a different extent the prices of X expected to rule at different future dates, and . . . . also . . . . the possibility that it may affect the expected future prices of other commodities or factors (both of these are serious omissions)."[6] Since it is precisely these "omissions" which are here at issue, there is no solution in this direction.

Besides observations and experiences bearing directly on the variables immediately affecting his business, the entrepreneur has available a great deal of evidence about broader market influences. General cyclical movements and tendencies in politics, in particular, are likely to be very important to him. That he studies such phenomena is abundantly plain from the content of newspapers and magazines addressed to businessmen.

Some of these events—such as elections, natural catastrophes, technical innovations—are "data" to the economist as well as to the businessman. But others—such as shifts in stock-market prices, behavior of such bellwether industries as automobiles and electric power, movements of foreign-exchange rates—are them-

[4] This consideration suggests that reactions to like divergences of experience from expectations may well be different in different phases of business fluctuations.

[5] Even this finding is somewhat weakened by the fact that "surprise" and "revision of anticipations" are inextricably intertwined (see below, pp. 85–86).

[6] *Value and Capital* (Oxford, 1939), p. 205.

selves economic phenomena. Unfortunately, however, even the
direction of the revisions arising from surprises in these fields is
not clear a priori. This is especially inconvenient since it is plain
that there must be important joint effects of these observations
and market experiences: in particular, outside data (both economic and political) must strongly influence the businessman's
view of the "normality" of an existing situation.[7] The problem
seems to the writer soluble in special cases but not in general—a
great handicap to analysis of business fluctuations.

II. COSTS OF PLANNING AND ESTIMATION AND THE ECONOMIC HORIZON

From the foregoing discussion it should be obvious not only
that the fullest information the firm can hope to obtain about future markets will be incomplete and unreliable but that to obtain
and use it will involve substantial costs. The information available about the plans of potential suppliers, customers, and competitors and about the factors which do—or should—underlie
those plans is copious but scattered. To collect from newspapers,
correspondence, and commercial and government forecasting
services all the information they contain would call for a vast
amount of clerical work. The resulting mountain of papers, moreover, would be useless unless competently digested and summar-
ized—which again is expensive.

Besides these costs of assembling data for estimation, there are
costs involved directly in the processes of estimation and planning
—in particular, diversion of the energies of business managers.
However thoroughly business organization may be systematized,
its efficiency involves a good deal of activity by the responsible
heads of the firm, both in supervising the conformity of current activity to plan and in bringing about those small adjustments of
provisional plans which in the aggregate are so important for
business success. Planning of later operations and estimation for
remote periods must be done at some sacrifice of present co-ordination and flexibility, unless the firm is merely projected and not yet
in operation; and in both new and old firms refinement of esti-

[7] Cf. J. A. Schumpeter, *Business Cycles* (New York, 1939), pp. 1038 ff.

mates and plans for one future interval must compete with estimation and planning for other intervals. In brief, the available supply of managerial services in a firm is likely—if not certain—to be too scant to carry estimation and planning for all dates to the highest pitch of perfection which could be obtained for any one interval if the others could be taken for granted. Here, as in other economic affairs, there is a margin beyond which a gain which would be very attractive, "other things equal," is not worth pursuing, because to do so involves sacrificing more important alternative gains.

Unfortunately it must remain eternally a matter of guesswork just where the margin of profitable estimation and planning lies. For it is impossible to tell accurately whether assembling more data and planning more carefully will yield enough improvement in income to pay for itself. To find out, rigorously, would require: (a) formation of a preliminary judgment from the most easily assembled data; (b) assembly of more data with leisurely revision of the preliminary judgment; and (c) submission of both judgments to the test of experience. To prejudge the difference, in an individual instance, after making the preliminary judgment, involves an accurate forecast both of the final estimate and of the event —which obviously cannot be made on the basis of the preliminary inquiry. Something can be done by comparing past experience under hasty judgments with past experience under estimates more carefully framed; but the experiences available are not normally entirely comparable.

Nonetheless, a choice exists between less unreliable estimates at higher cost and more unreliable estimates at lower cost; and a decision must be reached. Plainly, it would be as absurd to affirm that "rationality" in business calls for the most accurate estimates available regardless of cost as that it calls for the largest technically feasible output.

Two fairly general conclusions about rational planning and estimation flow from these considerations. The first is that it is likely to be irrational to have the general framework of the firm's plan continuously under revision, since to do so requires continuous attention from a number of the firm's leaders to the sacrifice of important details. Furthermore, some at least of the planning personnel are likely to be directors or consultants with outside interests which prevent being in continuous touch. Prudence will ordinarily leave adaptations to unexpected conditions up to a certain magnitude to subordinates, without continuous co-ordination. General revision need be undertaken only when the drift of market conditions away from expectations has accumulated to a serious extent—ordinarily a periodic meeting for planning will provide adequately for this—or when a major emergency comes up.

The second conclusion is that detailed estimation and planning for dates beyond the very nearest future is likely to be wasted effort. Even the course of events considered "most probable" will almost certainly diverge so from reality that all details of plans based on it will have to be re-worked. It is better economy to lay out only the broad outlines of estimates and plans for the distant future, concentrating attention on fields related to durable equipment whose acquisition must soon be considered. Somewhat more detailed plans are appropriate for the middle future (say a year or two ahead); and full detail is appropriate only for periods so short that losses from recasting plans are likely to outweigh losses from following faulty plans.

The two facts that the future is uncertain and that estimation and planning are costly combine to limit the range of the entrepreneur's view of the future. But his "economic horizon"[8] is not to be thought of as an absolute limit to his vision. Rather, there is a haze which obscures things more and more as they become more remote, but through which the larger features of the distant landscape can yet be made out—with greater effectiveness if expensive instruments are used. Estimates of the near future, and plans for the near future, may be so definite and detailed as even to be treated as single valued.[9] More remote events and opera-

[8] Cf. J. Tinbergen, "Notions of Horizon and Expectancy in Dynamic Economics," *Econometrica*, I (July, 1932), 247–64.

[9] The writer is informed that at R. H. Macy & Co. estimates of sales for each department are reduced to writing as single-valued estimates for each of the next four weeks. At the end of each week its experience is reviewed, estimates for the next three weeks revised, and an estimate for the fourth week framed.

tions cannot be seen with the same clarity; but we should not assume on that account that the entrepreneur has no ideas about them.

A product of the existence of a "horizon" in this sense is that the firm's capital value takes on a certain independence in the firm's estimates. In principle, the firm's net worth of course continues to depend on anticipations relating to future operations. But it is plainly more likely that an entrepreneur can find some way to equal or better an assigned net-receipts schedule than that he can do so by following any particular operating plan laid out in advance. Similarly, it is more likely that he can find a plan under which the present value of net receipts will equal or exceed a certain figure than that he can do so by following a particular schedule of net receipts. The capital value ascribed to some date in the middle future may thus be much more definite than the preliminary market estimates and provisional plans now in existence for operations beyond that date.

III. DISAPPOINTMENT AND REVISION OF ESTIMATES

If estimates were single valued, the concepts of disappointment and revision would be very simple and definite. Disappointment would mean a divergence between the experienced course of (say) a buying-price during the interval just passed and the previously anticipated buying-price schedule. Revision would consist in the substitution of a new single-valued buying-price schedule (for dates yet to come) for that included in the old set of estimates.

Not only would revision and disappointment be conceptually distinct; one could readily happen without the other. For example, receipt of unexpected information might lead to the setting-up of revised estimates even though experience had so far confirmed the old set. Or experience might diverge from estimates—for some definite reason applying only in the interval of the divergence, such as abnormal weather impairing theater attendance—without affecting future estimates.

With uncertain anticipations, however, the situation is more complex. As we have already seen,[10] the very core of the uncer-

[10] Pp. 55, 58–60, above.

tainty situation is the expectation of knowing more about the future as it draws in toward the present. In short, anticipations include the expectation that anticipations will change. Confirmation of initial expectations is not incompatible with revision of estimates; on the contrary, it implies a certain sort of revision.

To clarify ideas, it is worth stating the conditions for satisfaction of anticipations under uncertainty. If we consider estimates made at t_0 for the magnitude of a certain price at t_2, the entrepreneur's anticipations presumably include:

a) A probability distribution—which we may call $F_0(P)$—of possible prices, with an expectation value $E_0(P)$.

b) A set of contingent probability distributions which it is thought *may* exist at date t_1 (between t_0 and t_2). These we may call $F_{1,a}(P)$, $F_{1,b}(P)$, $F_{1,c}(P), \ldots, F_{1,n}(P)$; and their expectation values will be $E_{1,a}(P)$, $E_{1,b}(P)$, $E_{1,c}(P), \ldots, E_{1,n}(P)$. Each of these contingent distributions is assigned at t_0 a certain probability; their weighted sum will give $F_0(P)$.[11]

Certain necessary relations among these distributions can be traced. To begin with, no price can figure as possible under $F_0(P)$ which is not recognized as a possibility under at least one possible F_1. In the second place, the range of each F_1 will normally be much less than that of $F_0(P)$, and its concentration about the expectation value will normally be higher than that of $F_0(P)$. In the third place, the expectation will be at t_0 that the eventual F_1 will

[11] The situation is thus of the sort covered by the "law of compound probabilities." It may be illustrated by an arithmetical example, supposing for convenience that the different distributions are few and discrete, as follows:

PROBABILITY DISTRIBUTION OF SUPPOSED POSSIBLE PRICES

FUNCTION	PROBABILITY OF FUNCTION	E(P)	PROBABILITY OF PRICE OF—						
			0	1	2	3	4	5	6
$F_0(P)$......	1.00	2.875	0	0.1	0.275	0.3375	0.225	0.0625	0
$F_{1,a}(P)$	0.25	4.000	0	0.0	0.0	0.250	0.500	0.250	0
$F_{1,b}(P)$.....	0.50	2.700	0	0.10	0.30	0.400	0.200	0.000	0
$F_{1,c}(P)$.....	0.25	2.100	0	0.20	0.50	0.300	0.0	0.000	0

The probability of each price under $F_0(P)$ is the weighted sum of its probabilities under the F_1's; and $E_0(P)$ as computed from the F_0 distribution is identical with the weighted sum of the E_1's. In like manner, the F_1's may be thought of as weighted sums of estimates for distributions which might exist at dates between t_0 and t_1.

lie roughly in the center of the range of F_0 and will have an expectation value close to E_0.

Suppose now that the entrepreneur has estimates at t_0 for all future dates and that t_1 is a date (say) one month later. What must happen during the month in order to fulfil the expectations originally held? The following seem to be the necessary conditions:

a) Prices between t_0 and t_1 must follow the schedule of expectation values.

b) Estimates made at t_1 for each later date must have the same expectation values as estimates for the same date existing at t_0.

c) The t_1 estimates must recognize no possibilities for later dates not contemplated at t_0; and some of the more extremely favorable and unfavorable possibilities contemplated at t_0 must have dropped out of consideration (range must have narrowed).

d) t_1 estimates for each date must show higher concentration about the expectation than the t_0 estimates for the same date.

Conditions (*c*) and (*d*), it will be noted, are not stated in full rigor. The range and dispersion must not only have decreased but decreased in the expected degree.

While any of the conditions just listed may fail of fulfilment, only the first refers directly to market experience. Failure or fulfilment of the other three conditions depends not on the objective nature of events experienced but on their interpretation—whether the events are things in the firm's own market experience or outside it. In short, failure of condition (*b*), (*c*), or (*d*) means failure to revise estimates in the way expected.

Failure of condition (*a*) is the only case in which disappointment is really distinct from revision. Here—as under single-valued anticipations—disappointment may happen without revision following. If failure of this condition leads to revision, it must take the form of a contribution to the failure of condition (*b*), (*c*), or (*d*).

Failure of condition (*b*) means a revision of expectation values; and this is the one respect in which substantial revision of estimates is not expected. It may reflect some unexpected turn in events outside the firm's immediate sphere—an election, earthquake, court decision, real estate boom, or what not upsetting the basis of t_0 estimates. Alternatively, it may mean a failure of condition (*a*)—a divergence of market experience from expectations—which on examination reveals the presence of some factor which was neglected or underweighted in drawing up the original estimates. Either external or internal events, plainly, may lead to either optimistic or pessimistic shifts in expectation values.

Failure of condition (*c*) means the cropping-up of apparent possibilities not contemplated at t_0 or (in a less extreme case) failure of contingencies originally rated as fantastically unlikely to be written off the list of possibilities as expected.[12] Plainly, this is unlikely—though not quite inconceivable—unless there is failure of condition (*b*) or (*d*). If expectation remains unchanged, the range is virtually certain to remain unchanged if the dispersion of estimates shrinks. There must be a very freakish change in the structure of estimates—giving the curve embodying t_1 estimates a radically different character from that embodying t_0 estimates—to produce this effect. In any event, the range is a relatively unimportant aspect of the entrepreneur's distribution of estimates; so this question need not detain us.

Failure of condition (*d*) means a failure of the dispersion of estimates for dates beyond t_1 to shrink as expected. If the shrinkage of dispersion exceeds expectations, this will presumably reflect receipt of information unexpectedly early or in unexpected detail. If the shrinkage falls short of expectations (anticipations fail to converge), on the contrary, this will indicate delay in the receipt of expected information—or perhaps receipt of unexpected and unsettling information introducing new possibilities, such as rumors of war.

The factors just mentioned lie outside the firm's own immediate experience. But it is possible that the firm's own market experience may affect the dispersion of estimates unexpectedly. If the market experience between t_0 and t_1 is radically different from expectations (failure of condition [*a*]), the implication is likely to be not merely that some important element in the situation has been overlooked but that the firm's estimating procedure is at

---

[12] Cf. G. L. S. Shackle's note in *Review of Economic Studies*, October, 1940, in which the range of "likely" contingencies is treated as the only significant attribute of a set of uncertain estimates.

fault. This points toward less reliance on the expectation value of further estimates. Contrariwise, a period when condition (a) is almost perfectly fulfilled may enhance confidence in the accuracy of estimates. Strictly, we should say that the entrepreneur expects prices (etc.) not to follow but only to approximate expectation values.

Surprises which affect the expectation values of t_1 estimates will presumably act upon plans very much like surprises when estimates are single valued.[13] But surprises which affect also the dispersion of anticipations will also make the entrepreneur more or less anxious to preserve his firm's liquidity, to avoid investment in specialized durable equipment, etc.[14] There is thus a presumption that radical surprises on the firm's buying- or selling-markets between t_0 and t_1 will tend to encourage expansion of operations if agreeable, to encourage contraction if disagreeable, through effects on expectation values. The supplementary effect upon the dispersion of anticipations, however, is likely to be adverse to investment in either case.[15]

---

[13] See above, pp. 27–32. [14] See above, pp. 65, 68–71.

[15] For some of the implications of this line of argument for the theory of money and business cycles, see the author's papers on "Failure and Fulfilment of Expectations in Business Fluctuations" (*Review of Economic Statistics*, February, 1937) and "Consumption Markets" (*American Economic Review, Supplement*, March, 1938).

APPENDIX

THROUGHOUT this essay the entrepreneur has been supposed to plan with a view to maximizing the present discounted value of his expectation of net receipts. A number of other rules might have been adopted, however, including: (*a*) maximum discounted value of expectations of *withdrawals*, (*b*) maximum present net worth, (*c*) maximum income in the current accounting interval, and (*d*) maximum discounted value of expectations of income. The task of this section of the Appendix is to demonstrate the identity of these rules in the absence of capital-rationing and uncertainty.

To begin with withdrawals, it is plain that the present value of the withdrawal schedule is the (algebraic) sum of the values of the net-receipts schedule and financing schedule; for in each interval withdrawals equal net receipts plus financing. If the firm has no present debt, the financing schedule will have a present value of zero under all plans: for the present value of borrowings must obviously equal that of repayments (including interest). If it has some debt at present, the financing schedule has a negative value equal to the debt. In either case, its value is a constant in business calculations, not differing from plan to plan; and the plan offering maximum net receipts will also offer maximum withdrawals.[1]

The firm's present net worth, plainly, must in principle be regarded as the present discounted value of expected net receipts. Maximizing the latter is thus identical with maximizing the former; and rule (*b*) thus has no difference in content from the net-receipts rule.

[1] This assumes, of course, that outside capital will actually be repaid, with the rate of return promised. If (say) a noncumulative preferred stock issue is to be sold and the entrepreneurial group expects to pay out less in preferred dividends than the prospective stockholders expect, plans calling for such an issue will have an additional advantage as against other plans which is not represented in the comparison of prospective net receipts.

The current-income rule involves us in difficulties arising from the ambiguity of the term "income." To the economist, income normally means the amount that could be withdrawn from the firm during the interval in question, leaving its net worth unchanged, or—what comes to the same thing—the amount by which the firm's net worth would rise if nothing were withdrawn.[2] To the accountant, on the other hand, income normally means receipts from sales, minus operating expenses, depreciation, and maintenance. The two definitions do not coincide, as we shall see, unless special treatment is given to depreciation and maintenance; so that we must avoid assuming that all propositions which are correct under one definition also hold under the other.

Under the economist's definition, the plan offering maximum net worth will also necessarily offer maximum current income. Income under this definition is simply interest on the net worth. For if there are no withdrawals scheduled between t_0 and t_1, the t_0 net worth must be simply that of t_1 discounted back; and the increment of net worth (by simple inversion) simply the interest on the t_0 value.

On the other hand, under the accountant's definition the current-income rule does not make sense. It is common practice for firms voluntarily to undergo periods of low—or even negative— "net income" in order to win through to prosperity later on.[3] The present low income and later high income (or, in other circumstances, present high income and later low income) must be viewed together in deciding among plans. This points toward the discounted-future-income rule.

On close examination, it proves that the accountant's income concept permits exactly the same anticipated financial history to be interpreted by any of several variant anticipated income schedules, having different discounted values. The discounted-future-income rule cannot be taken seriously unless this ambiguity can be eliminated.

[2] See J. R. Hicks, *Value and Capital* (Oxford, 1939), p. 172; E. Lindahl, *Money and Capital* (London, 1939), pp. 144–46.

[3] As we shall see, this results from overconservative accounting practices regarding asset valuations and "good-will."

The source of the ambiguity lies in three accounting customs: (i) capital values are normally attributed only to physical assets, or at most to physical assets plus certain "deferred charges"; (ii) the gross (undiscounted) value of depreciation charges commonly equals that of the outlay (or book value) for the asset in question; and (iii) choice among depreciation formulas is more or less arbitrary.

Under these customs the selection of a depreciation formula affects the present discounted value of the income schedule. Since the near future is subject to less discount, present value will be raised by a shift of depreciation formulas which postpones charge-offs, reduced by one which accelerates them. True, the same shifts in formulas will also affect the present value of income streams representing alternative plans in the same direction. But there is no guaranty that the change will be in the same proportion; so that a real arbitrariness in choice of plans is involved. There are four possible ways to avoid this arbitrariness:

1. Conceivably some one depreciation formula may be shown to be logically required by the data of the given plan. In most circumstances this is not a very hopeful solution.

2. A combination of depreciation formulas may be sought which will always make the sum of asset values equal to the discounted value of net receipts. This really means abandoning the accountant's income concept and reverting to the net-receipts criterion.

3. Excessive (or inadequate) changes in the values of physical assets and deferred charges may be offset by appropriate changes in a "good-will" account. To all intents and purposes this is identical with No. 2.

4. A system of calculation may be adopted under which changing formulas does not affect present value. The way to do this is to charge as an expense compound interest on all book values of assets not yet written off. But if this practice is adopted, an ultra-severe depreciation formula under which all outlays are instantly written off in full will give the same present discounted value as any other. This formula, however, will reduce a series of sched-

uled net incomes to a series of scheduled net receipts. Hence anticipated incomes and anticipated net receipts must have identical present values.

Of all these alternatives, only the first one gives a rule which may diverge from the net-receipts rule in interplan comparisons.

II. INTERNAL RATES OF INTEREST AND THE PROFIT-MAXIMIZATION PROBLEM

The conclusions of chapter iii as to capital-rationing and the necessity of working out internal rates of interest may seem to contain an implicit refutation of the argument just concluded. The standard of maximum discounted value of net receipts seems to lose its clarity when the rates used in discounting are themselves results of the firm's policy decisions. But this inference does not stand close examination.

To begin with, the optimum plan is necessarily the plan which offers maximum present discounted value of net receipts by the criterion of the schedule of internal rates; this follows directly from the fact that under the optimum plan discounted marginal revenue of input is equal (not merely *proportional*) to marginal cost of input. There is no doubt, then, that the optimum plan under capital-rationing follows the maximum-net-receipts rule by the criterion of its own interest schedule.

But admitting that the internal-rate schedule is a guide to apportionment of resources once the general outlines of the plan it represents are determined, there remains a question whether the rule of maximum present value covers the rationing case. If we discounted at the borrowing-rate schedule, plainly, alternative plans under which net receipts would have a larger undiscounted aggregate but would flow in later might have larger present values.

One way out of this dilemma is simply to rule out all interest schedules as valuation criteria unless their application throughout the firm's calculations would give consistent results. On this basis the rule of maximum present value of net receipts would be supplemented by a rule of equality (rather than proportionality) between marginal costs and marginal revenues, and all schedules other than the internal-rate schedule would be excluded. But a liking for consistency is a matter of taste; so that an argument which does not insist on the disqualification of the borrowing-rate is to be desired.

Such an argument may be found by returning to the hypothesis that capital-rationing is absolute for the nearer future—that is, that the entrepreneur's withdrawal schedule is fixed for a few years ahead, and by going over for the nonce to the rule of maximum discounted withdrawals.

The present value of the firm's withdrawal schedule under any plan may of course be broken down into two components: the value of withdrawals scheduled for the period during which withdrawals are fixed and the value of later withdrawals, or—the same thing—the capital value for the end of the period for which withdrawals are fixed, discounted to the present. By hypothesis the first component is common to all plans; so that the plan offering the largest capital value for the end of the period is plainly preferable.

Of two unequal values available (say) five years hence, the larger must obviously have the larger present value at whatever rate we may discount. Since the optimum plan (as defined in the text) offers a larger capital value at the end of the period of absolute rationing than any alternative by the criterion of its internal rates, it must also be the optimum by the criterion of any other interest schedule that may be proposed.

This may be confirmed by considering the consequences of a marginal alteration away from the optimum plan (under which discounted marginal costs and marginal revenues are equal for all inputs). Suppose, e.g., that a dollar of expenditure is diverted, two years before the end of our five-year period, from input of two-year to input of one-year reaction interval. This will slightly raise the (undiscounted) marginal revenue of the two-year input and slightly lower the (undiscounted) marginal revenue of the one-year input. The resulting increment of receipts at the end of Year 4, by our hypothesis of absolute capital-rationing, must be reinvested, again at a slightly reduced marginal revenue of input. But previously the plan was so adjusted that a marginal dollar of expenditure at the end of Year 3 had the same effect on receipts at the end of Year 5 whether it went into two-year input or whether it went into one-year input and the proceeds were reinvested. Consequently, the transfer described will reduce the gross and net receipts of Year 5, leaving expenses and receipts beyond that date unaffected, and will mean a net loss by whatever schedule of rates we may discount.

Our argument so far has rested on the assumption of a fixed withdrawal schedule for the nearer future, which has released us from the necessity of considering the entrepreneur's time preference. We have now to generalize it.

As the entrepreneur adjusts his provisional plan through a series of approximations toward the optimum as defined in the text, he may find himself reducing his withdrawal schedule for the near future and thus raising his personal schedule of time-preference rates. If the time-preference rates are used for discounting, plans correlated with high rates will plainly tend to have low present values. Discounting each possible plan by the associated time-preference schedule, the highest present value will plainly be found at a lower scale of operations than is implied by the double rule of the text (i.e., equality of marginal costs and marginal revenues *and* equality of internal rates and time-preference rates); and the time-preference rates will lie below the internal rates.

This result, however, results from unfair application of criteria of valuation. To find that plan A is superior to plan B, when the first is judged by criterion A and the second by criterion B, is inconclusive. The same test (i.e., in this case the same interest schedule) must be applied to both plans. Any particular marginal adjustment of a plan, however, will bring only an inappreciable shift of time-preference schedules. Its desirability or undesirability will look the same either by the interest schedule appropriate to the base plan or by that appropriate to the modified plan. We may think of the approximation to the optimum plan as a chain of small adjustments, each of which is judged by the interest schedule arising after the last adjustment is made. Then we shall find plan B is preferable to plan A (of which it is a very slight modification) by criterion A (or alternatively by criterion B); plan C is preferable to plan B by criterion B (or by criterion C); on similar principles a further revision to plans $D, E, F, \ldots, N$ can be motivated. Now plan N may be preferable to plan A by criterion

N, while plan A is preferable by criterion A, and yet—by this chain process—the preferability of plan N to that which is preferable to plan A may be established.

III. DISCOUNTING SUBJECT TO CAPITAL-MARKET UNCERTAINTY

Where the capital market is uncertain, there is an accentuation of the difficulty just discussed—correspondence of different interest schedules to different alternatives under consideration. The difference is that when capital-rationing alone is in question the firm will choose *one* of these contingent situations; under uncertainty the firm can choose only *a range* of situations, the details of the outcome being determined by uncontrollable and unpredictable forces.

We may launch the argument, as before, by supposing the firm's withdrawal schedule frozen for some time ahead. The choices before the firm at the outset are primarily among different programs of dealing with durable goods; for the production schedule for the near future, together with corresponding inputs, will be approximately determined by existing plant and estimates. As in our former problems, we have now to decide which choice offers the largest expectation of net worth as of the end of the period for which withdrawals are frozen.

For simplification, we may suppose that plans are revised monthly and that the period for which the withdrawal schedule is frozen is two months. This implies that single-valued plans for purchases and operations are laid out for one month, with provisional plans (subject to revision at the end of the month) for the second month and later periods. Estimates must exist for the forecasts which may be held and the end of the first and second months.

Suppose the firm adopts plan (1) for the first month. At the end of the month, it may have estimate set A, B, C, ... , or N. To each estimate set (taken to include the actual price history and sales schedule of Month I) there corresponds a plan which would be adopted for Month II; these plans may be labeled $(1)A$, $(1)B$, $(1)C$, ... , $(1)N$. If the initial plan had been (2), the plan for the second month would have been $(2)A, (2)B, (2)C, \ldots, (2)N$,[4] and so on for other initial plans.

At the end of the second month, the external situation, as estimated, may have complexion $a, b, c, \ldots$, or n. In each of these situations, each of the possible courses of action labeled

$$(1)A, (1)B, \ldots, (1)N$$
$$(2)A, (2)B, \ldots, (2)N$$
$$\cdots\cdots\cdots\cdots\cdots\cdots$$
$$(K)A, (K)B, \ldots, (K)N$$

will have a capital value which for the moment we assume can be computed. For each initial policy there will be contingent capital values, each with a probability estimate attached and each having an expectation value which is the weighted sum of the contingent values. The initial policy for which this weighted sum is greatest should be followed. Since all these weighted sums are values of the same date (end of Month II), the interest rate used in discounting them back to the starting-point is immaterial.

The interest rates ruling within the two months (or the rationing-allowances granted the firm during those months) will, of course, influence the composition of assets both at the end of Month I and the end of Month II. In this sense they enter into the present value.

If in planning at the outset it is uncertain (say) what the firm's "line of credit" will be in Month II, different contingencies as to this event will be among the characteristics distinguishing the N situations recognized as possible at the end of Month I. If the firm's ability to reach capital is weak in Month II, the effects of initial plans which start buildings (e.g.) in Month I, to be completed with capital obtained in Month II, may be catastrophic. As we have seen in the text, initial plans with flexibility will be superior (allowing for all contingencies) to plans which involve such commitments.

But this is not confusing to the valuation issue. The device here used is essentially to break down the possible futures into

---

[4] Even though the *external* situation appears the same under $(2)A$ as under $(1)A$— as the notation implies—the firm's own history will have been different, and it will open Month II with a different outfit, according to its initial plan. The *total* situation $(2)A$ will therefore differ from $(1)A$, and so will the plans for the second month differ. Both internal and external situations under $(1)B$ differ from $(1)A$.

enough "contingencies" so that capital-market conditions may be regarded as certain within each contingency. Given the assumptions so far followed—possibility of valuation as of the end of Month II, and frozen withdrawal schedule meanwhile—uncertainty of interest rates down to the end of Month II does not affect the maximum-present-value rule of planning.

Previously, we have got rid of the difficulty of valuation by resolving capital values of a given date into the sum of a series of discounted later withdrawals and a discounted later capital value. But under the present assumptions this remedy is less satisfactory. If we wish to apply it to valuations at the end of Month II, we must extend the period for which the withdrawal schedule is frozen. Unfortunately, to freeze the withdrawal schedule involves implicit assumptions about net receipts and financing. Capital-market uncertainty implies that the financing schedule can be forecast only within limits, which grow wider and wider as the date for which estimates are made becomes more remote. Neglecting changes in cash balances, withdrawals of each date are the sum of net receipts from operations plus receipts from financing: the withdrawal schedule is the sum of the net-receipts schedule and the financing schedule. For a short period, possibilities of altering net receipts from operations to suit financing requirements, together with the slack afforded by cash balances, make it possible to guarantee a fixed withdrawal schedule. But, as the period stretches, there comes to be an appreciable probability that the financing schedule will take a form totally incompatible with the assumed withdrawal schedule.

We can get no further, in view of this difficulty, unless we can first free ourselves from the assumption of a frozen withdrawal schedule. Since the future cannot be fully predicted, it is plain that in operation withdrawals will be planned only contingently. (In fact, it is really easier to imagine a firm planning to maintain a frozen capital-value schedule by adjusting its withdrawal schedule than maintaining a frozen withdrawal schedule.) In essence, the value of the firm to the capitalist-entrepreneur under any given plan is the value of a set of contingent withdrawal schedules; and the market contingencies corresponding to each will indicate different interest schedules.

In principle, each of the contingent withdrawal schedules can be assigned a probability. If we could completely ignore risk aversion, it would be tempting to summate the contingencies into an expectation schedule and suppose that the plan would be selected whose expectation schedule of withdrawals (if certain) would have the highest value to the entrepreneur in his private capacity.

Even given its assumptions, this solution has difficulties. In particular, discounting to obtain a present value would not be simple. The writer can see no way to guarantee that the weighted sum of the contingent schedules of time-preference rates which would correspond to the different withdrawal schedules would coincide with the schedule of time-preference rates corresponding to the expectation schedule of withdrawals; and if not, no easy choice of interest rates for discounting could be made. It might be necessary simply to appeal to the preferences of the entrepreneur among withdrawal schedules, without trying to rationalize them into discounted values.

Since we cannot assume the nonexistence of risk aversion, the dispersion of the contingent withdrawal schedules about the expectation schedule (and the fact that under some contingencies withdrawal schedules will simply come to an end earlier or later with the firm's insolvency) cannot be ignored. But there is no tidy scheme for separating time-preference elements from risk-aversion elements; we must appeal to preferences among income prospects as wholes.

Going further, we are in still worse difficulties in case the "capitalist-entrepreneur" is a group representing several households. It is not logically necessary that the estimates of the members of the group should agree as to the composition or probability attributes of the income prospects offered by different initial plans. If they do not, we must assume either that "insiders" adjust operations affecting all to their preferences regarding their share or else that there is genuine economic indeterminacy in planning, the compromise among different interests being a political rather than an economic phenomenon.